NELSON T. GANT

NELSON T. GANT

**From Slave
to Prosperous
Business Owner
and
Respected Citizen**

LARRY SHIRER

Copyright © 2023 by Larry Shirer

All rights reserved. No part of this publication may be reproduced, stored or transmitted in any form or by any means: electronic, mechanical, digital, photocopy, recording, or any other—except for brief quotations in printed reviews, without permission from the publisher.

Author's website: larrysbooksandphotos.com

ISBN (hardcover): 979-8-9891882-0-8
ISBN (ebook): 979-8-9891882-1-5

Book design and production by www.AuthorSuccess.com

This book is dedicated to Phil Balderston, a compassionate Quaker from whom I learned much, but who passed away before I had a chance to learn all of what he had to teach, and to Steve Stewart who has ably kept the Gant story alive as president of the board of the Gant Foundation.

Contents

Introduction	1
Life on the Plantation	5
Challenges In Virginia	25
Life In Ohio	41
Life Lessons	93
Notes	107
APPENDIX A: Nelson T. Gant's Freedom Papers	111
APPENDIX B: Slaves Manumitted by Nixon Will	112
APPENDIX C: Nelson T. Gant Jr.'s Letter to His Classmates in 1931	113
APPENDIX D: Deed, Land—Convers to Gant 1865	114
APPENDIX E: Map of Underground Railroad Routes in Ohio	115
APPENDIX F: Sale Bill—Gant's Farm Tools and Equipment	116
APPENDIX G: Nelson T. Gant Timeline—Summary	118
APPENDIX H: Transcript of Interview with Victoria Robinson, Maria And Nelson's Great, Great, Great Granddaughter	120
APPENDIX I: Gant Family Tree	129
Acknowledgments	130
Will You Help?	131
Bibliography	132

Introduction

Nelson T. Gant didn't know how to quit. He had many opportunities to do so. On numerous occasions, the temptations to give up must have been nearly overwhelming. But giving up was not part of his nature. Born and reared a slave, he became a prosperous and respected citizen of an adopted community.

Nelson was born in 1821. He spent his childhood, teen years and early adulthood as "chattel," owned property, on a tobacco plantation in Virginia. While still a slave, Gant was married to a woman, also a slave, who was part of a household with a separate owner. Although married, they were not permitted to live together.

Gant was made a freed man by the last will and testament of his owner, who died in 1845, when Gant was twenty-four. His wife was still a slave. After being set free, Gant labored in Virginia for a while to raise money to "buy" his wife, but her mistress refused his initial efforts to purchase her freedom. He vowed not to live without his beloved and promised he would return for her.

Nelson traveled to Pennsylvania and then to Ohio, to join the other freed slaves from the Virginia plantation where he had labored, who had settled near Zanesville.

He soon resumed his efforts to become reunited with his wife. His return to Virginia was marked by adventure and challenges, including arrests, two court appearances and a further indictment. Both he and his wife spent time in jail.

After arriving in Ohio, Nelson got a job, saved his money, bought some land, became a farmer, eventually accumulated over 300 acres of land and owned and operated four businesses. He assumed civic responsibilities, became a respected citizen, provided major support to his church, served as a university trustee, and was active in the Underground Railroad.

The Nelson Gant story is really three stories. There is a romance story within an adventure story, and then a "rags to riches" story. The book is organized into five parts. Part one is the introduction. Part two describes the life of Gant and others like him who grew up enslaved. It attempts to give the reader a glimpse of what it was like to be a slave. Part three recounts the obstacles and issues with which Nelson had to deal, and how he dealt with them. Part four describes how he became a wealthy and prominent citizen in Ohio and a conductor on the Underground Railroad. Part five identifies the character traits and strategies for overcoming adversity that enabled him to achieve so much.

I became involved in the Gant project almost by accident. I grew up just outside of Zanesville. When we "went to town" it was to Zanesville. As a teenager, I played American Legion baseball in Municipal Stadium, which is now called Gant Municipal Stadium. I frequently stayed with my grandmother, who lived in Zanesville. I still have relatives there, but live in another part of the state. I am a history buff, an author, and a photographer. Before learning of Gant, I had self-published six books and had five more on my to-do list. One of the projects on my list was to write a book about the role of Ohio, and particularly of Zanesville, in the Underground Railroad. I did some preliminary research on the internet and came across references to Gant.

During a visit to Zanesville for a funeral, I decided to visit the former home of Gant on West Main St., just outside the city limits.

The home is now owned by the Nelson T. Gant Foundation and serves as a tourist attraction and educational center. It is listed as an Underground Railroad Site by The National Park Service and the Underground Railroad Network to Freedom. I was reading the plaques in front of the building when a man drove up in a red pickup truck. He introduced himself as the vice president of the Gant Foundation and asked me if I would be interested in seeing the home. I said sure, and he showed me around. While we were touring, another man came in. He turned out to be the president of the foundation. The two shared with me the highlights of the Gant story. I was intrigued.

Over the next few days, I conducted some additional research about Gant. I found numerous bits and pieces of his story, with lots of gaps and several inconsistencies, but no comprehensive accounts. Upon reflecting on my conversations with the two gentlemen at the foundation and the research I had done, I was hooked! I concluded that it would be much more interesting and useful to tell the Gant story than to produce another "me too" book about the Underground Railroad.

I called Vice President Ware and requested a meeting with him and President Steve Stewart. They agreed. At the meeting, I proposed that I write a book about Gant that they could sell in their gift shop. They asked that I outline my proposal at the next meeting of the board of directors, which I did. The board graciously approved the project and we were off and running.

Gant's story is an impressive and inspiring account of an extraordinary person, the adversities he faced and overcame, and his many achievements. I have attempted, based on my research and experiences, to identify the character traits and the strategies for overcoming adversity which enabled him to accomplish so much. He was a remarkable man. The story reveals lessons from which we all can learn.

In reflecting upon my feelings about the project, I was motivated to tell a story that was important and that could inform and inspire a larger audience, if it were more widely known. I confess that I was also motivated by sharing a sense of shame and guilt that the race of which I am a part so cruelly treated a group of humans of another race, because they were "different" and considered "inferior." If this work in any small way helps to increase the understanding of the evils of prejudice and discrimination and provides just one person with the hope of, the understanding of, and the requirements for overcoming adversity, it will have been worth the effort.

Life on the Plantation

Birth

Gant's life was marked by drama from the beginning—literally. His mother died giving birth to him. Family lore relates that she fell, gave birth and died on the path from the slave quarters to the "big house."

Nelson Talbot Gant was born on a 240-acre tobacco plantation near Leesburg, in Loudoun County Virginia, on May 10, 1821 (or in some accounts 1822). His mother was a slave on that plantation. There is no known record of either her first or last name. He was informally adopted and reared by Edith, Eva or Eve Gant, another slave on the same plantation, whose last name he took as his own. Nelson's manumission papers list him as a mulatto, (half African American and half white).

In a blog about Gant's marriage, Victoria Robinson—Gant's great-great-great granddaughter, wrote that: "His descendants have carried down a story of his birth in which Nelson was the half white son of his owner and who was orphaned when his slave mother died giving birth to him."[1] Ms. Robinson cites as the source of this information an interview with Margaret Goss Winn, Gant's great-granddaughter.

Ms. Robinson, who has done a lot of research about Gant, indicates more recently that tests of her and her mother's DNA link them, not to the owner of the plantation where he was born, but to a famous white preacher of the Leesburg area, who was also a slave owner, an ardent defender of slavery and a vocal opponent of abolitionist activities.[2]

An article in the Zanesville, Ohio *Courier* of November 22, 1894, indicates that when, as an adult, Nelson's foster mother suggested that he might want to use his father's surname rather than hers, he adamantly refused, stating that his father would not acknowledge him when he was a boy, and that he was pro-slavery, so he would not consider using his father's name.

The Plantation

The owner of Woodburn Plantation, when Gant was born, was John Nixon, the son of George, who immigrated from Ireland. George had obtained title to the land in 1777, by filing a "patent" and building a

Woodburn Grist Mill built by George Nixon in 1777. The mill has been converted to a residence. It, the nearby Miller's Cabin, and five acres were for sale in 2023 for a mere $1,225,000.

16' X 20' log cabin on it, which was the requirement for obtaining title. The same year, George built a gristmill on the property. His initials and the 1777 date appear on a "date stone."

John had the main house built around 1820. Because of the elaborate size and design, it was dubbed by locals as "Nixon's Folly." The handsome, thirteen room, Federal style, two-story brick home was built by William Benton, who later built the Oak Hill Estate for President James Monroe, just a few miles away.

The following description of the property is included in the application for listing in the National Register of Historic Places:

> *Woodburn, located among the rolling hills of Loudoun County, contains a remarkably well-preserved collection of eighteenth and nineteenth century domestic, agricultural and industrial buildings, representing several phases in the evolution of a large Northern Virginia farmstead.*
>
> *The main house is a two-story, five-bay, gable roofed structure with an interior end chimney on the west end and with double interior chimneys connected by a parapet on the east. Built of brick laid in Flemish bond on the south and west sides and in four-and five-course American bond on the north and east sides, the house has an original seven-bay, two story ell. The ell, too, is built of brick laid in four-and five course American bond and projects off-center from the rear of the main house.*

An unusually ostentatious barn was added at about the same time. The large, four bay bank barn is also of brick, with jack arches and molded brick cornices to match those of the house.

The Nixon's had wealth and built structures to demonstrate it. The entire Woodburn building complex is listed in the National Register of Historic Places.

The Woodburn Estate Main House, built for George Nixon circa 1820. Where Nelson served as manservant to John Nixon.

The Woodburn Estate barn, built circa 1820.

The Early Years

As a boy, Gant had chores on the plantation, but found time to play, hunt, and fish with the other boy slaves.

On the plantation, Gant was called Talbot. Records show various spellings of his middle name. His emancipation papers spell it Talbert. Maria's manumission papers list her as "wife of Talbut Gant." An 1847 letter is signed as Nelson Talbourt. Other records show it as Talbott and Talbot.

Because he was bright, courteous, conscientious, and a diligent worker, Gant became a favorite of John Nixon. Young Gant became a personal manservant, or valet, to Nixon, which meant he labored in the "big house" rather than in the fields.

The role of manservant typically involved serving as personal attendant to a master, caring for his wardrobe, helping prepare and serve his meals, cutting his hair, shaving his whiskers, and generally serving as the master's "right hand man" and "gofer." The role generally carried with it greater trust than was typically afforded a slave, so Gant ran errands and assumed responsibilities greater than those normally assigned to a slave. A manservant was at the master's beck and call and seldom far from his side. Gant accompanied Nixon as he directed work on the plantation and as he conducted his business affairs with outsiders. This experience helps explain how Gant developed the skills that later served him well as a businessman.

His role may also explain why and how he learned to read and write. There were laws in Virginia and other slave states that stipulated that it was illegal to teach a slave to read or write. Gant demonstrated great proficiency in both abilities in later life. John Nixon may have chosen to overlook the law, to make Nelson more useful to him, or Nelson may have learned later.

Growing Up Enslaved

Nelson Gant's achievements would be impressive for someone who had experienced a "normal" childhood. For someone who was enslaved, another person's owned and controlled property until he was age twenty-four, and someone of a race still considered inferior by many, even after slavery, what he accomplished is astonishing.

Psychologists tell us the experiences of the formative, "growing up" years are significant determinants of the kinds of adults we become. For many, the experience and psychological trauma of growing up enslaved was debilitating. Nelson, however, learned from his experiences and used them to motivate him to excel.

Implications of Being a Slave

For those of us who have never experienced the condition, it is nearly impossible to imagine what a slave's life was like. To really appreciate Nelson's achievements, it is helpful to understand a little about the realities of life as an enslaved person.

The enslaved were denied basic rights we take for granted; the

---

Virginia "Black Laws"

African Americans in Virginia were subject to a different set of laws than were people with white skins. The following are examples of the many laws specific to slaves and/or African Americans. The dates listed are the years the laws were enacted.

- A punishment is provided for loitering runaways in the colony; for a second offense a runaway is to be branded in the cheek with the letter "R." 1642.
- Stealing a slave is a felony, and the punishment death without benefit of clergy. 1732.
- A slave shall not go from where he lives without a license of letter showing he has authority from his master. 1785.

- All meetings of slaves at any meeting house or any other place in the night shall be considered an unlawful assembly, and any justice may issue his warrant to enter the place where the assembly may be for apprehending or disbursing the slaves, and to inflict corporal punishment on the offenders at the discretion of the justice, not exceeding twenty lashes. 1804.
- If any slave hereafter emancipated shall remain within this Commonwealth more than twelve months after his freedom, he shall forfeit such right, and may be sold by the overseers for the benefit of the poor. 1806.

right to move from one place to another (they had to have a pass from the owner to go anywhere off the plantation), adequate nourishment, safety, shelter, education, health care, and clothing; freedom from fear and, perhaps most critically, respect as a human being. Slaves, of any age, could be sold, bought, separated from families, starved, worked to death, tortured, crippled, or killed, with no consequences for the perpetrator. They were property, just like a cow or a plow subject to the whims of the owner.

Slavery flourished in the United States for nearly 250 years. At the end of the Civil War, there were over four million slaves in America. More than a fourth of those were under sixteen years of age. Conception was encouraged because it was more profitable to raise slaves than to raise cotton. Some owners specialized in raising slaves to sell.

By design, slaves were taught shame and humiliation, that they were inherently inferior. The intent was to "keep them in their place." One recalled his feelings as a child:

> *My recollections of early life are associated with poverty, suffering and shame. I was made to feel,*

- Because of serious inconvenience experienced by Virginians from the frequent elopement of slaves to states north of the Potomac it is enacted that hereafter $20.00 reward, and mileage, be allowed any person who may apprehend any runaway slave attempting to cross the Potomac. If the slave is apprehended in Maryland or Kentucky, the reward shall be $25.00; in Delaware, New Jersey, Pennsylvania, Now York or Ohio, $50.00, plus twenty-five cents a mile. 1817.
- Any white person who shall intermarry with a Negro, or any Negro who shall intermarry with a white person, shall be confined in the penitentiary from two to five years. 1878.

in my boyhood's first experience, that I was inferior and degraded, and that I must pass through life in a dependent and suffering condition.[3]

Enslaved women and girls lived with the fear of being sexually abused. That their fears were justified is evidenced by the fact that, according to the 1860 census, of the over four million persons identified as blacks, over 600,000 were classified as mulatto, i. e. of mixed black and white races. That number is probably low as slaves were often inaccurately counted.

The law prohibited sexual relations between races. Religion held that fathering children outside of wedlock was a sin. The existence of mulatto children served as a constant reminder that the fathers had broken the law and violated the tenants of morality. That they represented such evidence, meant that mulatto children often suffered even more abuse than entirely black slave children.

The Importance of Family

Family bonds were one of the few sources of solace available to slaves.

Parents attempted to shield their children from some of the atrocities of slavery, but their ability to do so was limited. For children, the love of parents and extended family was the only glimmer of pride and self-respect they experienced. Children and parents lived in constant fear of becoming separated. Owners believed that they had the right to dispose of property as they pleased, and, as a result, children were sometimes split from their parents. Historians estimate that more than half of the slaves in the United States were sold multiple times during their lives, each time leaving family and loved ones behind. Moses Grandy relates what happened when one of his brothers was sold:

> *My mother, frantic with grief, resisted their taking her child away. She was beaten and held down. She fainted, and when she came to herself, her boy was gone. She made much outcry, for which the master tied her up to a peach tree in the yard and flogged her.*[4]

In 1841, Solomon Northrup, an educated, Afro-American citizen of New York state, with a wife and children, was enticed to travel to Washington D.C., on the promise of a gig as a musician. In Washington, he was kidnapped and shipped to Louisiana, where he was enslaved on a cotton plantation until freed in 1853. In his book, *TWELVE YEARS A SLAVE*, Northrup recounts a scene he witnessed at a slave trader's facility in New Orleans:

> *I have seen mothers kissing for the last time the faces of their dead offspring; I have seen them looking down into the grave, as the earth fell with a dull sound upon their coffins, hiding them from their eyes forever; but never have I seen such an exhibition of intense, unmeasured, and unbounded grief, as when Eliza was parted from her child.*
>
> *She broke from her place in the line of women, and rushing down where Emily was standing, caught her in her arms. The*

child, sensible of some impending danger, instinctively fastened her hands around her mother's neck, and nestled her little head upon her bosom. Freeman sternly ordered her to be quiet, but she did not heed him. He caught her by the arm and pulled her rudely, but she only clung the closer to the child. Then, with a volley of great oaths, he struck her such a heartless blow, that she staggered backward, and was like to fall. Oh! how piteously then did she beseech and beg and pray that they might not be separated. Why could they not be purchased together? Why not let her have one of her dear children? 'Mercy, mercy, master', she cried, falling on her knees. 'Please, master, buy Emily. I can never work any if she is taken from me; I will die.'

. . . Finally, after much more of supplication, the purchaser of Eliza stepped forward, evidently affected, and said to Freeman he would buy Emily, and asked him what her price was.

'What is her price? Buy her?' was the responsive interrogatory of Theophilus Freeman. And instantly answering his own inquiry, he added, 'I won't sell her. She's not for sale.

The man remarked he was not in need of one so young—that it would be of no profit to him, but since the mother was so fond of her, rather than see them separated, he would pay a reasonable price.

But to this humane proposal Freeman was entirely deaf. He would not sell her then on any account whatever. 'There were heaps and piles of money to be made of her, he said, when she was a few years older. There were men enough in New Orleans who would give five thousand dollars for such an extra, handsome, fancy piece as Emily would be. No, no, he would not sell her. She was a beauty—a picture—a doll—one of the regular bloods—none of your thick lipped, bullet-headed, cotton-picking niggers.'

When Eliza heard Freeman's determination not to part with Emily, she became absolutely frantic. 'I will not go without her. They shall not take her from me', she fairly shrieked, her shrieks comingling with the loud and angry voice of Freeman commanding her to be silent. . . . . Finally, out of patience, Freeman tore Emily from her mother by main force, the two clinging to each other with all their might.

'Don't leave me mama—don't leave me', screamed the child, as its mother was pushed harshly forward; 'don't leave me—come back mama' she still cried, stretching forth her little arms imploringly. But she cried in vain. . . . Still we could hear her calling to her mother, 'come back—don't leave me—come back mama', until her infant voice grew faint and still more faint, and gradually died away, as distance intervened, and finally was wholly lost.[5]

Food

Interviews with ex-slaves frequently mention that children often went hungry. There was never enough food for the under-productive. The owner determined the weekly allotment per person. There was meat only if the men and boys were successful in hunting. Some families were allotted small plots for gardens because that reduced the owner's costs.

On many plantations, while the parents were in the fields, the children were fed in groups from troughs, like the pigs. The fare was often "mush," a mixture of corn flour and water, flavored with molasses. They ate with their hands or with crude spoons fashioned from seashells. The effects of malnutrition were common.

Healthcare

Doctor care for a slave was rare. Diseases and injuries were treated by elder slaves who practiced folk medicine passed down from ancestors in Africa. For "medicine," they used what they could find, from herbs, roots and bark. Infant and child mortality rates for slave children were twice those for the white population.

Typically, other slaves assisted slave mothers giving birth. There was no attending physician when Nelson entered the world.

Work

Some children were put to work at the age of five or six, others at ten or twelve. There were abundant chores for children. They carried firewood, carried water, fed the chickens and livestock, scrubbed the floors, picked worms off the crops, served as scarecrows in the gardens and fields, pulled weeds, swept porches and paths, and cared for younger children. They often spent hours fanning their masters and their guests to keep away the flies and mosquitos, and to provide relief from the heat.

Becoming a full-fledged field hand, at about age twelve, was a mixed blessing. It meant receiving the same amount of food as an adult and perhaps better clothing, but it also meant grueling work for long hours. During harvest time, slaves were expected to work the fields from sunrise to sunset, often fifteen hours or more per day.

Education

Slaveholding states passed laws stipulating that it was illegal to teach a slave to read and write. Slaveholders feared that education would prompt slaves to become dissatisfied with their plight and run away or revolt. In spite of the laws, some became literate. They learned from: white children who didn't know about the laws, from other slaves who had somehow acquired the skills, from parents who had somehow developed the skills, and from well-meaning white folks.

In his book: *Narrative of the Life of Frederick Douglass, An American Slave,* Douglass recounts that the wife of one of his masters taught him the rudiments of reading. When his master learned of his wife's attempts, he severely scolded her, saying:

"Learning would spoil the best nigger in the world. If you teach that nigger how to read, there would be no keeping him. It would forever unfit him to be a slave."[6]

His comments sum up the reasoning behind the anti-literacy laws.

But Douglass had discovered what he describes as "the pathway from slavery to freedom." He had the spark and he fanned it into a flaming passion to become literate. He relates that he took bread from the kitchen and would trade it to the poor white kids in the neighborhood, "who, in return, would give me the more valuable bread of knowledge."[7] He indicated that he learned to write by secretly perusing and copying lessons in the schoolbooks left about by the son of his owners.

Slaves who acquired such skills were taught to hide them. Slaveholders did not appreciate literacy among slaves. There are reported cases of owners cutting off the fingers of slaves who had the audacity to write. Children who aspired to acquire literacy skills were taking a lot of risks. They were secretly motivated to prove they were as intelligent as white kids and reasoned that if learning to read and write was open to white kids, but forbidden for them, it must be a good thing.

Nelson apparently shared Douglass's passion for literacy for he demonstrated adept skills for reading and writing in later life, although it is not clear how he developed the skills.

CLOTHING

Boys and girls were provided the same piece of clothing, a long shirt with a hole for the head and two for the arms. For the boys the garment was called a "shirttail" and for the girls it was called a "shift." Typically, young people were not provided underwear. Shoes for youngsters were rare. Adults were typically provided one set of clothing for summer and one for winter.

Toys

Purchased toys were an inconceivable luxury. Boys rode stick horses and girls played with dolls fashioned from rags, sticks, and string.

Housing

Slave quarters were typically one-room shacks with dirt floors, in which the whole family ate, slept, and lived. The most common configuration was a ten- or twelve-foot square with one door, no windows, and a fireplace. Any furnishings were crude affairs built from scraps by the residents. The "homes" were cold in winter and hot in summer. Outhouses were not usually provided, so all residents relieved themselves in the surrounding bushes, woods, or fields.

Many believe Josiah Henson was the model for the character, "Uncle Tom," in Harriet Beecher Stowe's novel. In his autobiography, he describes living conditions on the plantation in Maryland where he was enslaved:

> Our dress was of tow-cloth ... a pair of coarse shoes once a year. We lodged in log huts ... wooden huts were an unknown luxury. In a single room were huddled, like cattle, ten or a dozen persons, men, women, children ... There were neither bedsteads nor furniture ... Our beds were collections of straw and old rags ... The wind whistled and the rain and snow blew in through the cracks, and the damp earth soaked in the moisture till the floor was miry as a pig sty.[8]

Community

On some plantations the slaves attempted to affirm their humanity by forming a sort of underground culture. They gathered in the evenings in the slave quarters to tell stories, sing songs, share values with the children, and teach them how to cope. They might even make each other laugh by imitating the antics of their white masters and mistresses.

Religion

Some slaves turned to religion for inspiration and hope. The concept that there was a better life after this one was of some solace. Some practiced Islam and other religions they had brought from Africa. Some shared Christian beliefs, but with definite African twists. They typically rejected the Christianity professed by their masters, because it was used to justify slavery.

Punishment

Some slaveholders devised cruel punishments to instill obedience and fear in their slaves. Young people, owned by such masters, grew up witnessing and experiencing brutal treatment, often for the most trivial offense. Henry Bibb, an ex-slave who escaped from Kentucky, related that his "infant child was frequently flogged, for crying, until his skin was bruised literally purple."[9]

The whip was the symbol of slavery. The punishment most practiced was whipping, lashing or flogging with switches or straps. Paddles were sometimes employed. Broken bones from physical blows or kicks were not uncommon. In some instances, children were branded with hot irons. Other slaves, including children, were often compelled to watch the punishment. Slaveholders believed that demonstrations of extreme cruelty would frighten the other slaves into submission.

In Northrup's narrative, he tells of the lashing of Patsey, a slave who, without permission, had visited the mistress of the adjoining plantation. After being stripped of all her clothes and tied face down to four stakes in the ground:

> *The painful cries and shrieks of the tortured Patsey, mingling with the loud and angry curses of Epps, loaded the air. She was terribly lacerated—I may say, without exaggeration, literally flayed.*

> *The lash was wet with blood, which flowed down her sides and dropped upon the ground. Her screams and supplications gradually decreased and died away into a low moan. She no longer writhed and shrank beneath the lash when it bit out small pieces of her flesh. I thought that she was dying. Finally, he ceased whipping from mere exhaustion.*[10]

In his *NARRATIVE*, Frederick Douglass relates the following experience of witnessing punishment and his feelings about it:

> *He was a cruel man, hardened by a long life of slaveholding. He would at times seem to take great pleasure in whipping a slave. I have often awakened at dawn of day by the most heart-rending shrieks of an own aunt of mine, whom he used to tie up to a joist, and whip upon her naked back till she was literally covered with blood. No words, no tears, no prayers, from his gory victim, seemed to move his iron heart from its bloody purpose. The louder she screamed, the harder he whipped; and where the blood ran fastest, there he whipped longest. He would whip her to make her scream, and whip her to make her hush; and not until overcome by fatigue, would he cease to swing the blood-clotted cowskin. I remember the first time I ever witnessed this horrible exhibition. I was quite a child, but I well remember it. I never shall forget it whilst I remember any thing. It was the first of a long series of such outrages, of which I was doomed to be a witness and a participant. It struck me with awful force. It was the blood-stained gate, the entrance to the hell of slavery, through which I was about to pass. It was a most terrible spectacle. I wish I could commit to paper the feelings with which I beheld it.*[11]

Overseers were often the administrators of punishment. One overseer reportedly explained to a visitor that negroes were sometimes determined to resist attempts by a white man to whip them. In those cases, there was no choice but to kill them.

The following photo of a slave named Gordon was published in Abolitionist brochures and widely circulated in their campaigns against slavery.

The ultimate punishment was murder, often in the form of hanging a victim by the neck until dead. These lynchings were often public celebrations designed to instill fear among African Americans and to affirm white supremacy. Some victims were accused of crimes no more serious than failing to show a white person the respect and deference he or she felt they were owed. Not all masters and overseers were brutal, but the relationship between them and their slaves never approached equality. Most slaves learned at an early age to expect pain and punishment as a fact of life.

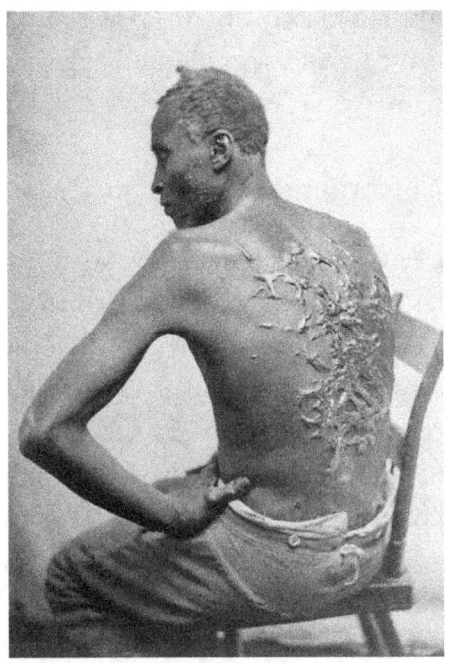

Photo of Gordon, a slave on a Louisiana Plantation, circa 1863. This photo was widely circulated by abolitionists in their anti-slavery literature.

Nelson—An Exception?

Although, in a letter, Nelson referenced experiencing the "horrors of slavery," we have no evidence that he was physically abused or harshly treated on the Nixon plantation. He was probably treated more humanely than the typical slave, but the psychological burden of being raised a slave meant that he had more than the typical obstacles to overcome, in order to live a productive and respectable life.

Nelson and Maria

Eve Gant had a daughter, younger than Nelson, named Winifred Jane. Winifred was permitted to attend a Colored Sunday school class at the Leesburg Methodist Church. She was dedicated enough to walk the three miles to the church in Leesburg. The class was conducted by Deacon Samuel Gover. There, Winifred became friends with a "dark mulatto" slave girl, from Leesburg, named Anna Maria Hughes.

Anna Maria, at about age three, was among a group of slaves gifted by Sarah Elizabeth (Betsy) McCarty Russell to her three daughters. The daughters—Eliza, Sara Elizabeth and Charlye Ann Elizabeth Jane Russell, never married. The Russell ladies lived in Leesburg. They had some prominent neighbors including Charles Eskridge, the Clerk of Courts of Loudoun County, the attorney for the Commonwealth of Virginia and John Janney, a noted Quaker lawyer. Anna Maria, when she matured, became the personal "house" servant of Charlye Ann (Jane).

It is probable that Nelson met Maria through Winifred. He was smitten. Initially, Charlye Ann discouraged Nelson's advances, indicating she thought he was not good enough for "her" Maria. Nelson persisted. Their relationship developed. Charlye Ann relented and the couple married in the Russell home, with the consent of both owners, on May 11, 1843. Nelson would have been twenty-two and Maria seventeen. The marriage was conducted by a Methodist Minister, probably the then Reverend Samuel Gover, who had led the class for Colored youth that Maria and Winifred had attended.

Although married, the couple could not live together. They continued to reside in the homes of their respective owners and to carry on their duties as slaves.

Nelson is Freed

One of the most articulate and outspoken abolitionists of the period, Lydia Marie Child, visited Leesburg in 1842 and spoke at a meeting about the evils of slavery. She had written a book in 1833 titled *An Appeal in Favor of that Class of Americans Called Africans*. That book was the first anti-slavery book printed in America. In it she stated that "The intellectual inferiority of the negroes is a common, though most absurd, apology for personal prejudice."

John Nixon was impressed by her and by her arguments condemning slavery. Soon after that experience, he changed his will to provide for the freedom of his slaves upon his death. In addition to their freedom, his slaves were to receive sufficient funds to pay for their travel to a free state. Nixon had no direct descendants. The Nixon's only child, a girl, died at a young age. The death of his wife preceded his.

John Nixon died in 1845. In September of that year, Nelson T. Gant and twenty-one other Nixon slaves received their manumission documents, emancipating them from slavery.

Nelson was free!

A copy of his Freedom Papers are shown in Appendix A. The names of the other Nixon slaves, freed at the same time, are listed in Appendix B.

Challenges In Virginia

Nelson was free. Free to go where he pleased as long as he left the state of Virginia within twelve months of the date of his manumission. The proponents of slavery did not want freed slaves hanging around to remind those still in captivity that there was an alternative. So the legislature passed a law stipulating that if a freed slave was still in the state twelve months after being freed, he/she could be apprehended, sold and returned to slavery.

Attempts To Free Maria

Maria, however, was still the property of Miss Russell. Nelson did not want to leave without her. He appealed to Miss Russell to free Maria, stating that he could not leave nor live without his beloved. Miss Russell denied his request.

Nelson resolved to buy Maria's freedom. He responded to a newspaper solicitation for woodcutters and entered into a contract to cut 500 cords of wood, along the Potomac River, at the rate of 40¢ per cord. It took the better part of a year to fulfill the contract. He returned to Miss Russell with the funds he had accumulated and offered to purchase his wife, saying, "He could not live in the West without the person who was more dear to him than all the world."[12]

Miss Russell refused, indicating that the money he had saved was not enough to buy Maria.

Nelson left, but promised Maria that he would return for her.

He headed for Muskingum County, Ohio, where Eve Gant, his foster mother, and several other of the freed Nixon slaves had settled. On the way, he made the acquaintance of a Dr. Julius LeMoyne in Washington, Pennsylvania. Dr. LeMoyne was a white medical doctor and philanthropist who was an active abolitionist, member of the American Anti-Slavery Society and conductor on the Underground Railroad. A subsequent letter from Gant to Dr. LeMoyne references Gant's stay at LeMoyne's home and indicates that they had developed more than a cursory friendship. LeMoyne probably directed Gant to other "safe houses" along the way, to help him reach Zanesville unmolested. Gant's letter also mentions a Dr. Delaney of Pittsburg, to whom Lemoyne had apparently referred him. Lemoyne may also have encouraged him to contact abolitionists in the Zanesville area, such as A. A. Guthrie and his brother George. Subsequent developments indicate that Gant developed relationships with the Guthries and other abolitionists in the Zanesville area.

Gant returned to Loudoun County, Virginia, in October of 1846, determined to somehow free Maria. He again attempted to purchase Maria's freedom with funds he had borrowed in Ohio. Miss Russell again refused. Nelson later related that Miss Russell's overseer threatened to kill him if he came near the house again.

Maria, while "on loan" to Miss Russell's neighbor Charles Eskridge, the Loudoun County Clerk of Courts, turned up missing. Mr. Eskridge, belatedly informed Miss Russell that Maria had disappeared. He sent her this note:

> "Your servant Maria eloped from my house the night before last, and the law makes it my duty to give you notice of the fact, and to advertise her in some public newspaper, which I shall do in our next paper.
>
> Yours Respectfully,
> Chas. G. Eskridge"

(Note that this is the same Charles Eskridge who had signed Nelson's freedom papers.)

Nelson related, in an article printed in the *Cincinnati Enquirer* of January 21, 1879, the story of his and Maria's adventures over the next few weeks. The next few paragraphs are a summary of that story.

They met outside Leesburg and headed to Washington, D. C. They walked the approximately forty miles. Gant related that he carried Maria on his back a good part of the way. Nelson had been referred, probably by the people in Putnam, Ohio, or by LeMoyne, to the home of someone in the Underground Railroad, who would help them.

They reached the address to which they had been directed, tired and hungry. Their potential benefactor met them at the door with tears in his eyes and begged them not to get him involved. He indicated that he could not help them because he had been arrested a few days before and placed under a $4,000 bond, to appear in court on charges of aiding another runaway slave. He said he was under constant surveillance and pleaded with them to go away before they got him into trouble. He gave them the name and address of an African American man who would help them.

Betrayal

They went to the address of the second man and were received cordially. But instead of shelter, they found betrayal. They were exhausted and starving, having been afraid to stop on the way to seek food for fear of being apprehended. They gave this man some money to go buy food for them. He left, supposedly to buy food, but returned with six policemen. Nelson and Maria were arrested. Nelson was determined to resist with pistol and knife, but Maria dissuaded him and they were taken to jail.

We can only speculate about the motive of the betrayer. It was likely greed or fear and probably the former. It was not uncommon for rewards to be offered for information leading to the abduction of runaway slaves.

Nelson had some forged freedom papers for Maria that he had brought with him from Ohio. Upon examination, those papers were found to be fake. Maria and Nelson spent thirteen days in a Washington DC jail, while Nelson awaited trial. Then, through the efforts of Miss Russell, the Governor of Virginia had them extradited back to Leesburg for trial. Nelson was bound hand and foot and thrown on top of a stagecoach for the trip to the Leesburg jail.

Maria spent twenty-two days in the Leesburg jail before being returned to her mistress. During that time efforts were made to convince her to admit that Nelson had induced her to run away with him. Nelson later related that she told him she was confronted by one of the Russell sisters with the threat of being turned over to a slave trader and sold "South," unless she testified that Nelson had enticed her to run away. She stuck to her story that she had decided on her own to run away and that Nelson had learned of her departure and followed her.

According to an article in the *Zanesville Courier* on November 22, 1894, Maria's mother urged Maria to testify against Nelson so she would not be sold and shipped south. Maria's reply was: "No. My husband was free and he risked his freedom and life for me, and I shall die before I testify against him."

Nelson arrived at the Leesburg jail in late October and was charged with "carrying Maria out of state in order to defraud and deprive her owner of Maria's $500 value."[13]

The Virginia criminal code stated that the punishment for stealing a negro slave was confinement in the state penitentiary.

Nelson paced a cell in the Leesburg jail, a place he described as loathsome, for weeks. The court met only once per month. The trial was scheduled for November. It convened, but was promptly postponed at the prosecutor's request, because of his futile attempts to convince Maria to implicate Nelson and his unsuccessful

CHALLENGES IN VIRGINIA   29

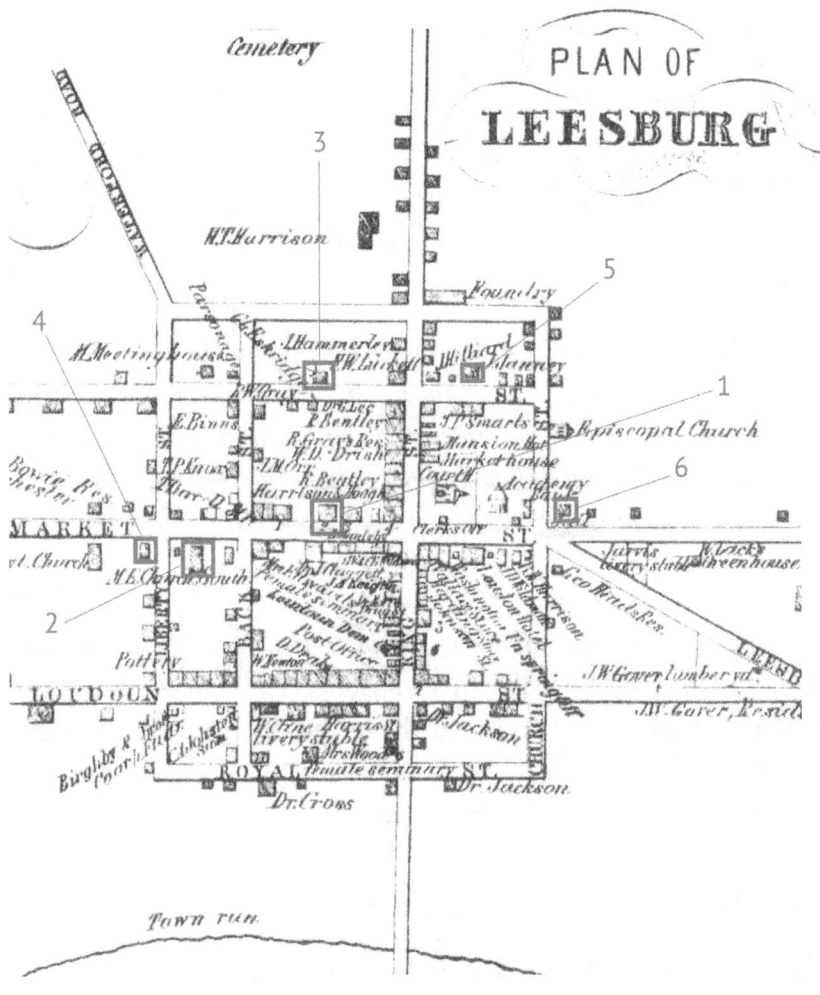

Map of Leesburg, Virginia, circa 1840.

1. The Russell home where Maria lived and served.
2. Church where Anna Maria and Winifred Jane went to a Sunday School class
3. Home of Clerk of Courts Charles Eskridge, who signed Nelson's manumission documents and where Maria was working when she "ran away".
4. Courthouse where Nelson was tried for "stealing" Maria.
5. Home of John Janney, the Quaker lawyer, who led the defense team for Nelson's trial and acquittal.
6. Jail where Nelson was confined while awaiting trial.

attempts to find other credible witnesses. So Nelson had to wait to learn his fate.

Nelson became despondent. He related that during the wait, he was informed by one of his attorneys that he would surely be convicted at the next term of the court. Nelson faced the real possibility of being separated from his beloved forever. He was out of money and nearly overcome by despair.

> *Then God raised me up a true friend in my trouble. Thomas Nichols, a worthy Quaker, for whom I had once done some insignificant service, came into the jail one day and handed to me through the bars a roll of money, saying he could not sleep while I lay there; that if I got out, I was honest and would repay him, and that if not, he could well spare the money.*[14]

Nichols had been the executor of John Nixon's will and had accompanied and assisted the freed Nixon slaves in their immigration to Ohio. He persuaded his friend, the respected Quaker attorney and abolitionist John Janney, to defend Nelson. Janney was assisted by Robert P. Swann and James S. Carper.

The Trial

The case came to trial on December 9, 1846. Maria and Nelson had a lot at stake.

No transcripts of the trial have been found, but several newspapers covered it. The *National Era* of Washington DC, on January 7, 1847, the *Christian Register* of January 30, 1847, The *Baltimore Visitor* of February 3, 1847, and the *New York Evangelist* of February 11, 1847, all reported the major legal arguments recited by the attorneys.

Swann initiated the defense by stating that "Nelson was a man "united in holy wedlock to a woman for whom he has evinced the strongest feelings of attachment. Although his skin wears a different hue from ours, we cannot doubt that the feelings of his heart are the same. Their vows have been registered in the chancery of Heaven; and shall we attempt to set the laws of man above the Divine law, by separating those whom God hath joined?"[15]

White wives were exempted by law from testifying against their husbands. Slave marriages were not recognized by the courts. A key legal point in this case was the issue of whether or not Marie could be compelled to testify against Nelson. Carper argued that since they were married, she could not be ordered to testify.

The prosecutor argued that slaves were not persons, but property, and thus Maria was not protected by the law that applied to whites. He insisted that it would be "manifestly absurd to recognize a relationship of this kind which interferes with the legal rights of the master and contradicts all the laws which are made for the security of his property."[16]

The prosecutor called a "jet black negro man" who he alleged had seen Nelson near Leesburg the morning of the day Maria disappeared. Upon

Fugitive Slave Laws

The United States Congress passed two federal laws that permitted and facilitated the capture and return of runaway slaves. Nelson was prosecuted for violating the Fugitive Slave Act of 1793, by allegedly "stealing" his wife Maria while she was still a slave. That law authorized local governments to capture and return refugee slaves to their owners and imposed punishments on anyone who abetted the runaways in their flight.

Most significantly, it declared that the owners of slaves and their agents (slavecatchers) had the right to pursue and search for refugee slaves within the borders of free states (and Washington D. C.). The law also imposed a $500 fine on anyone who concealed or assisted a runaway slave.

Many citizens of Northern States criticized the law, claiming that it legalized kidnapping and turned their states into grounds for "bounty hunters." In fact, the law did result in many free Blacks being kidnapped and sold as slaves. One famous such case was that of Solomon Northrup, a free citizen of New York State. Northrup was kidnapped in Washington D. C. in 1841, shipped to Louisiana and enslaved for 12 years, before obtaining his freedom in 1853. He wrote a book about his experience entitled TWELVE YEARS A SLAVE. The book was made into a movie, which won the Academy Award for best movie of 2013.

Representatives of the Southern States pressed for more stringent federal measures. In an attempt at appeasement and to calm threats of secession, Congress passed the Fugitive Slave Act of 1850. This law attempted to force ordinary citizens to assist in the apprehension of refugee slaves. It stated that: "All good citizens are hereby commanded

cross examination, the witness stated: "I say to George I think it was Talbott, but when he no speak to me I don't know whether it was Talbott or not. Being airly in the morning, not fairly light, I could not tell whether it was a black man or a yellow man. Dat's all I know about it."[17]

His testimony was dismissed as non-conclusive.

Janney took the ground that Maria was the lawful wife of the prisoner, married with the consent of her mistress, at her mistress's house, and with the implied consent of the prisoner's master—united in the bonds of matrimony by a minister of the gospel; and he repeated what had been said by his colleague in the opening of this case—that their marriage was "registered in the chancery of Heaven."

The opinion expressed by our opponent, that slaves cannot be married according to law, would tend to the general corruption of morals and the most enormous abuse. Can it be possible that the whole colored population of Virginia are living in a state of concubinage? No! It is the intention of the law to promote public morals, not to degrade them. It is intended to throw a shield around innocence, and to punish only the perpetrators of crime. Maria is the lawful wife of the prisoner; and it is a point well established, that in a case like this, the testimony of a wife cannot be taken either for or against her husband. The reason is obvious: it would present so great an inducement to perjury that no court would be justifiable in subjecting a human being to so strong a temptation.[18]

By Nelson's account, Janney made an eloquent speech, lasting six hours. Nelson related, in the later *Cincinnati Enquirer* article, that it was the most affecting scene he ever witnessed, that the courtroom was crowded and Janney brought tears into everyone's eyes.

Janney's appeal was so powerful that Presiding Justice Saunders said: "The poor boy has done nothing. Let him go."[19]

The five-judge panel ruled that Marie did not have to testify against Nelson. The court dismissed the case against Nelson and he was released from jail. The decision was unprecedented. No previous court verdict had ever recognized a slave marriage. The judges on the panel were apparently moved to do what was right, rather than adhere to the letter of the law.

to aid and assist in the prompt and efficient execution of this law."

It also increased the punishment, for anyone assisting a runaway, to a fine of $1000 and six months in jail. The law also prohibited a refugee slave from testifying in her or his own defense.

In a few cases, abolitionists demonstrated their disapproval of the law by affecting the release of apprehended slaves by physical force. In 1851, a group of abolitionists in Boston stormed the courthouse, freed Shadrach Minkins from custody and led him to sanctuary in Canada. Similar "rescues" occurred in other states, including one in Oberlin, Ohio. The Fugitive Slave laws gave birth to the Underground Railroad and became virtually unenforceable in several Northern States.

Both Fugitive Slave Laws were repealed by Congress on June 28, 1864.

Sketch of the Loudoun County Courthouse where Nelson's trial was held.

The Loudoun County Courthouse that replaced the one in which Nelson's trial was held.

Maria's Freedom

Nelson was free again, but Maria was still in bondage. He again appealed to Miss Russell, pointing out that she had given assent to their marriage. She again refused.

But public opinion had shifted. A group of the prominent men of Leesburg visited her and told her that if she would not sell Mrs. Gant to Nelson, they would not be responsible for the consequences. She finally relented. Maria's manumission papers were recorded on February 8, 1847.

According to the letter Nelson sent to LeMoyne in June of 1847, he paid $775 to Miss Russell for Maria's freedom, half again as much as the value the court had placed on Maria when they charged he had stolen her. He indicated in the letter to LeMoyne that he had borrowed money from Thomas Nichols and "friends in the west." Nelson had legal fees to pay as well as the money he borrowed to buy Maria's freedom, so they were burdened with debt. Mr. and Mrs. Gant elected to stay in Virginia to work at paying off the obligations there.

Settling Virginia Debts

Again, Nichols stepped up. According to a publication called *A Nest of Abolitionists*, Nichols and his wife Emily opened their home in Circleville, Virginia to the Gants in 1847, and provided them with employment. In Nelson's 1847 letter to LeMoyne, he indicated that LeMoyne should send any reply correspondence to him at Circleville, Virginia, where Nichols was the postmaster.

The Nichols home in Circleville, Virginia, where Nelson and Maria lived and worked after the trial to pay back Nichols the money he loaned Nelson when he was in jail.

The following is a transcript of Nelson's letter to LeMoyne:

7th of June 1847

Respected Friend

According to the promise I made your wife whilst at your house last fall I will now try to fulfill. I have seen and felt much of the horrors of slavery since that time. I found many friends in Pittsburgh among them Dr. Delaney who I consider one among the finest of men with their assistance I reached Chambersburg and from thence directly to Loudoun my old home, and from there to Washington where I met my wife. We were directed to a colored man's house and were betrayed by him and thrown into prison where my wife was kept 8 days and I was kept 13 days and stood a short trial. Then the case was removed to Leesburgh for further trial my wife was confined in Leesburgh jail 22 days and threatened by one of her owners to be sold to the far south if she did not testify against me this she refused to do then we were taken to court and they tried to force her into measures but she would only say she knew nothing about it and would tell nothing. My lawyers pleaded on the ground that we were lawfully married and with the consent of our master and mistress and upon these grounds we were acquitted by the county Court.

The lawsuit and purchase of my wife amounts to upwards $775 with the assistance of my friends and borrowing about $225 from Thomas Nichols all is settled but the money I borrowed. My wife and myself are both working with Thomas Nichols. My Brother in Law in the west and several other friends intend to assist me some and I hope it will not be long before we reach a land of Freedom. When we do come we intend calling on you. Give my respects to your wife and also remember me to Dr. Delaney of Pitts, and Judge Leever of West Middletown.

Before I close I must assure you I shall never forget with what kindness I was received by your wife and I hope I still retain a place in your memory. With this short history I will now bring my letter to a close. Accept my best respects and believe me to be

Your humble servant

PS please write soon and direct your letter to Circleville Loudoun, Va

Nelson Talbourt Gant[20]

Tax records indicate that Nelson and Maria lived parts of 1848, 1849, and 1850 with the family of Samuel Janney. After they paid the money borrowed from Nichols, they still owed money for legal fees and additional amounts borrowed to purchase Maria's freedom. Samuel offered Nelson and Maria employment and a place to live. Samuel Janney and his wife operated the Springdale Boarding School for Girls in Lincoln, Virginia. Nelson and Maria worked at the school. The couple's first child, Mary Elizabeth, was born during this period.

Sketch of Springdale Boarding School for Girls, where Nelson and Maria lived and worked from 1848 to 1850.

Photo of the Springdale School, 2023.

Samuel was a cousin of John Janney, the attorney who represented Nelson at his trial, and also a friend of Thomas Nichols. Samuel was a Quaker, of the same Goose Creek Quaker Meeting as Nichols and his cousin John. An ardent abolitionist, he wrote and spoke out against slavery fervently and frequently. At one point he was arrested on the allegation that some of his writings were intended to encourage slaves to rebel. He was acquitted of the charge.

More Legal Problems

Nelson's legal problems were not over. In 1848, while laboring to pay his debts, he was indicted for exceeding the twelve-month limit of the time an ex-slave could stay in the state after being freed. His trial for that charge was repeatedly postponed and the charge was finally dismissed in June of 1850. In that same month a certificate of freedom for Mary, the twenty-month-old daughter of Maria and Nelson, was registered.

After the charges were dropped, in late June of 1850, Nelson, Maria and Mary departed Loudoun County for Ohio. They probably visited with the LeMoynes on the way because they didn't arrive in the Zanesville area until fall.

Life In Ohio

Beyond The River

Free at last to leave Virginia, Nelson and Maria found their way to Ohio in the fall of 1850. They headed to Muskingum County, because that was where several of the slaves from the Nixon plantation, including Nelson's foster parents, had settled. The 1850 census indicates that Nelson's foster parents were living on a farm in Monroe Township, in the eastern part of Muskingum County, and that his foster-brother and his family were living in Falls Township, near where Nelson's family ended up.

The two largest settlements in their "Freedom Land" were Zanesville and Putnam.

Zanesville

Ebenezer Zane founded Zanesville in 1800 and established a ferry to transport goods and people across the river. The first ferry consisted of boards lashed atop two canoes to provide a surface for passengers and cargo. The new town was named in Zane's honor in 1801. Zane had a contract with the federal government to blaze a trail from Wheeling, (West) Virginia to Maysville, Kentucky. That trail, originally only wide enough for horses in single file and later widened to accommodate wagons, was known as Zane's Trace. The Wheeling to Zanesville section eventually became part of the "National Road," the first federally financed highway. That road originally stretched from the Potomac River at Cumberland, Maryland to the Mississippi River at Vandalia, Illinois. Later, additional sections were added as US Route 40 extended coast to coast.

Zane's payment for building Zane's Trace was three parcels of land with 640 acres each. He deeded the parcel that included Zanesville to his brother Jonathon and his son-in-law John McIntire, in payment for their assistance with the project. McIntire settled in, and played a major role in building, Zanesville.

Because of its strategic location on Zane's Trace and at the confluence of the Muskingum and Licking Rivers, Zanesville prospered as a trading and industrial center. River transportation was less costly than overland transportation. From Zanesville, the Muskingum flowed to join the Ohio River at Marietta. The river location thus provided access to markets for Muskingum County goods in Marietta, Pittsburgh, Cincinnati, and beyond.

Zanesville became the second capital of Ohio from 1810 to 1812.

Zanesville is best known for its unique Y Bridge. The first version of the Y Bridge was a covered bridge, built with a center pier of limestone, and wooden and stone trestles, to which logs and planks were bolted. It connected all banks of the Licking and Muskingum rivers. When it opened as a toll bridge in the fall of 1814, the tolls were as follows:

> Each foot passenger—3 cents
>
> Horse, mule or ass, one year old and upwards—4 cents
>
> Each horse and rider—12 ½ cents
>
> Each sleigh or sled drawn by two horses or oxen—25 cents
>
> Each coach with four wheels and driver, drawn by four horses—75 cents

The Zanesville Covered Y Bridge circa 1814. Sketch by the author's grandson Kyle.

When Nelson and Maria arrived in 1850, Zanesville had a population of approximately 8,000 persons. Muskingum County, of which Zanesville is a part, had a population of close to 45,000, of which approximately 600 were of African American heritage.

While Nelson is associated with the city of Zanesville in many accounts, the home where he and Maria reared their family was, and still is, outside the city limits.

Putnam

It is probable, that Nixon and/or Nichols chose Muskingum County, Ohio as a refuge for the Nixon ex-slaves because of the reputation earned by the community there called Putnam.

The village of Putnam, originally called Springfield, was established in 1800, before Ohio was a state. Founded and laid out by Increase Mathews and Levi Whipple, the village was renamed in honor of Rufus Putnam, one of Ohio's preeminent pioneers. It was located on the banks of the Muskingum River, across that river from Zanesville. The two settlements were divided by more than a river. Conflicting attitudes about slavery prevailed in the two communities. The settlers of Zanesville were predominantly pro-slavery Kentuckians and Virginians. Many of the settlers of Putman were abolitionist New Englanders. Some were Quakers. Putnam was referred to as a "hotbed of abolitionists."

When Nelson and Maria arrived in Muskingum County in 1850, the population of Putnam was approximately 1,500.

Working For Convers

Shortly after they arrived in Muskingum County, Nelson became employed by Theodore Convers, in the farm produce business. A Zanesville Times Recorder article dated July 15, 1905, just after Nelson's death, indicates that the Gants rented a home from Convers after arriving in the area. No record of an address for that home has been found.

It is likely that Nelson was connected to Convers by A. A. Guthrie, a Putnam abolitionist. Nelson had apparently hooked up with Guthrie on his first visit to Ohio. He had mentioned to LeMoyne, in an 1847 letter, that he had borrowed money to purchase Maria's freedom from friends in Ohio, likely from Guthrie and his associates.[20]

Guthrie and Theodore's brother, Charles Cleveland Convers, were associates. They jointly purchased the land for Woodlawn Cemetery and both served on the board of directors, (as Nelson did later). Charles was a lawyer and politician. He served as Speaker of the Ohio Senate and as a judge on the Ohio Supreme Court.

Theodore was also an attorney. For a while, he and Charles were partners in a law firm. Theodore also owned and operated a soap, candle and lard manufacturing business. The relationship between Theodore and Nelson was apparently cordial. Theodore died in 1855, at age thirty-five. In his will, Theodore wrote:

> *Should Nelson Talbot Gant be in my employ at the time of my demise, but not otherwise, I give and bequeath to him my gray horse John, should I own him at my demise, and also any one of my cows he may select. This bequest I make as a token of my appreciation of his honest and faithful devotion to my interests.*[21]

One of the Gant children, who was born and died at the age of five months, in 1855, (the year Convers died), was named Theadora or Theadore, apparently as an indicator of the Gants' regard for Convers.

Nelson later purchased 142 acres of land from Catherine Convers, the widow of Charles Cleveland Convers, who was the brother of Theodore.

Family

Nelson and Maria were devoted to each other. Nelson asked a beautiful mulatto slave to "travel down life's pathway with him, hand in hand, to rejoice with him when success greeted his efforts, and to sympathize with him when misfortunes came."[22] He credits Maria with standing with him through trials and tribulations, and for setting him on the Christian path. At great risk to body and freedom, he vowed that he would not live without her by his side. He begged Miss Russell, at least three times, to free Maria so they could be together.

Nelson, when freed, could have fled to a free state and left Maria in bondage, but his love, affection, and dedication prevented him from doing so. Nelson chopped wood for nearly a year in an effort to attain the money to buy Maria's freedom.

That love, dedication and affection was reciprocated by Maria. Maria made a home for him, bore him children, acted as hostess to his friends and business associates and abetted his Underground Railroad activities.

The impressive marble monument in Gant Circle of Woodlawn Cemetery is this man's testament of love for the woman who bore his children and completed his life. The inscription at the base of the monument reads as follows:

"Loved by Her Family, Respected by her Neighbors, Cherished by Her Church. This monument is erected as a token of her Husband's Love."

Monument to Maria on Gant Circle of Woodlawn Cemetery in Zanesville.

Inscription on Monument to Maria.

Anna Maria

Maria demonstrated her loyalty and devotion to Nelson when she repeatedly declined to implicate him in a conspiracy to induce her to flee Leesburg, even when she was threatened with being turned over to a slave trader if she refused.

Her spiritual faith was important to her. Nelson credits her with bringing him to God.

She was a helpmate and supporter to her husband, a devoted mother, manager of the household, and gracious hostess to guests. She took great pride in the three daughters and one son she helped rear to adulthood and mourned the early loss of her other children. She encouraged her children to become well educated and saw that they had music lessons, just like the kids of rich white folks on Southern plantations. She sold strawberries and cream from her front porch, along with milk and butter from her cows, to supplement the family income.

Maria showed appreciation for the liberties of freedom, was a compassionate contributor to the community and an active member of the South Street A.M.E. church.

She died while visiting her daughter Sadie, her son-in-law and her grandchildren at Yorktown, Virginia, in October 1877.

In a eulogy written by Bishop Daniel Payne upon her death, he described Maria as one sustained by religious beliefs. He proclaimed that she was zealous of good works for the church, the poor, and the needy regardless of background.

Payne wrote of one example of her compassion:

> *She was equally diligent in her visitations to the sick, and ready to relieve the wants of the poor without respect of race or color. A remarkable instance of this character was revealed soon after her death, in the testimony of an Irish woman who went to Mr. Gant to inquire if the report of his wife's death was true. Having been informed of its certainty, she broke into bitter lamentations, saying 'O that good woman is gone! She's gone! She's gone! When I was in need of some money to buy me a cow, that I might have wherewith to get food for my children, I went from house to house to borrow what I needed, but no one would loan me; then I came to Mrs. Gant; I told her my wants, she took out her purse and putting nineteen dollars in gold in my hands, said she 'take this money and if you ever be able, pay me back; if not, then, I give it freely to you.*[23]

Payne's tribute went on to say:

> *Her easy circumstances never make her proud and haughty toward those of her neighbors as were less favored by fortune. On the contrary, she was humble and not condescending. She was sweet tempered, so that she was always affectionate toward her husband, and entered heartily into all his plans of usefulness. Her children shared largely in her love, so that her husband and children really*

loved her because she was lovable; her neighbors knew how to respect her because she was hospitable and generous; her church knew how to cherish her, because she was a diligent and successful worker.[23]

Bishop Payne concluded the eulogy by citing a letter of condolence received by Nelson from a Mr. Daniel W. Atwood, who, at the time, worked for the Government in Washington, DC, but had earlier been a school principal in Zanesville. Atwood had been a close friend of the Gants and thus well aware of the attributes of the deceased. The letter attests to the esteem in which she was held by those who knew her. He wrote:

My Dear Sir:

Trusting that you have sufficiently recovered from the shock caused by the unexpected announcement from a distance, of the sudden death of a loving wife, a devoted mother, and a faithful, consistent Christian, to realize the fact that you have suffered one of the severest bereavements in life, and that really you are without the aid and council of one who, above all others, was a source of comfort in your riper years, I have taken up my pen . . . to perform a duty which I feel I owe to you, and the memory of your dear wife.

Allow me then, sir, to assure you, that my heart was touched with profound grief, upon hearing of the sudden death of Mrs. Gant, a woman in whom I always found a friend—one who, though weary with the toll of many years, and worn with labors which knew no hours, was ever ready to do a friendly act or go on an errand of mercy. Now that such an one, crowned with duties well done, is beckoned by the shadowy hand. . . it is decorous that those who are soon to follow her should pause, and bear testimony of the esteem in which they beheld her, and of the approbation which they know she deserved.

Though my words cannot add aught to her good name, they will,

> *I trust, serve to strengthen and brighten the links which bind us, friends together. I beg to remind you that though the decedent has entered the dark valley of death, . . . yet her passage was illumined by the rays of Christianity, and she has realized ere this, that it is not darkness the Christian goes to at death, for God is light; that it is not an unknown country for her, for Jesus is there, and the vast company of the just made perfect.*[24]

The newspaper notice of Maria's death included the following:

> *Mrs. Gant lived many years in our midst, and her kindness of heart, lady-like deportment and Christian virtues endeared her to all her neighbors, both white and colored. She leaves the partner of all her joys and sorrows, and early struggles, to mourn her loss. She was a loving wife during all their long years, whether surrounded by trials and misfortune or by prosperity, ease and comfort. She was a devoted mother to her children, who now mourn her loss.*[25]

The Gant Children

Several accounts mention that Maria and Nelson had twelve children. We can find records for eight. Only four lived to become adults—Mary Elizabeth, Sarah (called Sadie), Margaret, and Nelson Jr. Theadora, died at five months and Henrietta at ten months. Benjamin lived for only four days. Alice died at age five. Maria took great pride in the lives of her surviving children and mourned the deaths of those she lost.

Some of the deceased children are buried in the Dillon family cemetery, developed by Nelson's Quaker friend John Dillon, near the Gant home. While the Muskingum County grave records list Theadora, a girl, the headstone in Dillon Cemetery reads "Theadore, daughter of."

Sadie married Daniel McNorton, an ex-slave who escaped to New York in the 1850s. He became a medical doctor and moved back to Virginia after the Civil War. He there served on the State

LIFE IN OHIO 51

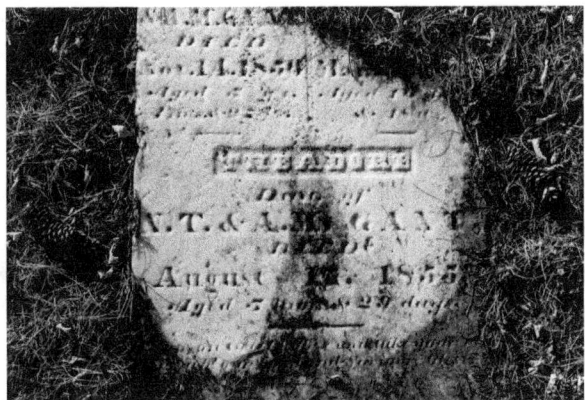

Gravestone for Theadore Gant in Dillon
Cemetery near the Gant Home.

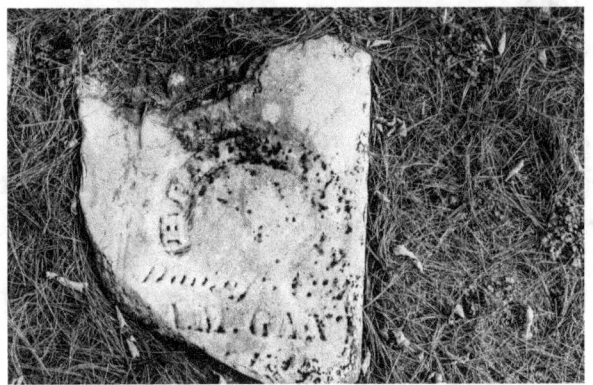

Gravestone for Benjamin Gant in Dillon
Cemetery near the Gant Home.

Memorial on the Dillon Cemetery near the Gant Home,
where the Gant children who died young are buried.

Constitutional Convention and was elected a member of the Virginia State Senate, where he served for twelve years.

Mary Elizabeth married Robert Manley of Zanesville and helped manage her father's affairs. They lived in a home Nelson had built for them on the Gant farm, just west of his home.

Margaret married George Potts of Williamsburg, Virginia. They lived in Yorktown, Virginia for a while and then moved to Zanesville, where Potts started a pottery company.

Nelson Jr. was born in 1867. He was enrolled in the preparatory department (high school) of Oberlin College in 1880, was registered as a college freshman in 1885 and graduated with a Bachelor of Arts degree in 1889.

Nelson Jr. was apparently recognized as a gifted student. An article in the *Zanesville Courier* in August of 1888 relates that when the professor of the Greek class, of which Nelson was a member, was taken ill, an Oberlin administrator entered the classroom and informed the students that since the professor was ill, Nelson Jr. would be teaching the class until the professor returned.

Nelson Jr. worked with his father in the family business until 1890, when he accepted a position in the State Insurance Department in Columbus. An article in the *Zanesville Times Recorder* of July 13, 1900, includes the following:

> *Nelson T. Gant sr. has purchased a handsome residence on Twenty-first Street, Columbus, Ohio, for the use of his son, Nelson T. Gant, jr., who is a clerk in the office of the commissioner of insurance.*

In 1892, Nelson Jr. married Florence Mintzing of Baltimore. The couple had no children.

A copy of a letter from Nelson Jr. to his Oberlin classmates, written in 1931, is included in Appendix C.

Nelson and Florence are buried in Gant Circle of Woodlawn Cemetery.

Gravestones for Nelson Jr and Florence Gant on Gant Circle of Woodlawn Cemetery.

Nelson and Maria valued education. The four children all were provided with music lessons and became accomplished musicians. They performed at family and community gatherings. Three of the four studied at Oberlin College, the first white college in the country to accept African American students.

"Aunt Sarah"

In the mid-1850s, the Gants retained the services of a young white girl who had emigrated from Lincolnshire, England to Muskingum County with her family in 1852. Her name was Sarah Speed and she lived with the Gant family until her death in 1921. The 1860 Federal Census shows her living with the Gant household as a "boarder." The 1870 census indicates that she was living at the Gant residence as a "bookkeeper." The 1880 census lists her as a "domestic servant."

Victoria Robinson indicates that she recalls that her grandmother Winn talked of Sarah as a "nanny" and housekeeper who was considered a part of the family and was referred to by the grandchildren and great grandchildren as "Aunt Sarah." Sarah stayed on in the Gant household after Maria's death and moved in with the Gant's granddaughter, Mariah Black, after Nelson died.

Her close association with the family is affirmed by the fact that her grave in Gant Circle of Woodlawn Cemetery is marked by a gravestone reading "Aunt Sarah Speed."

Gravestone for Sarah Speed on Gant Circle of Woodlawn Cemetery.

Nelson's Second Marriage

While traveling, Nelson met Lavinia J. Neal of Parkersburg, West Virginia. Despite a difference of thirty-seven years in their ages, they were wed in January of 1879. The ceremony took place at the home of the bride's foster parents, Mr. and Mrs. Julies. It was not at all similar to Nelson's previous ceremony in Leesburg. The *Zanesville Courier* reported that:

> *About 100 of the best people—white and colored—of Parkersburg were present at the ceremony and reception. It may be stated here that the wedding gifts were so numerous and valuable that their intrinsic value is estimated at $1,500, besides a check for $500. The trousseau was extensive and beautiful beyond our powers of description.*

The following day the couple traveled to Nelson's home near Zanesville, where a second lavish reception was held.

The death of a stillborn son from this union, on October 15, 1880, was recorded in Lavinia's family bible.

Nelson and Lavinia had one daughter, Lavinia Logan, (called Lulu). Lulu graduated from Lash High School in Zanesville. According to an article in the Zanesville newspaper, under the heading; "Colored Society Notes," Lulu was the only colored graduate of the class of 1900. During the commencement exercises, Lulu acted as accompanist and won many laurels for the quality of her playing. Lulu later graduated from the Boston Conservatory of Music.

High School Graduation portrait of Lulu Gant, daughter of Nelson and Lavinia.

She married Dr. E. H. Gee of Zanesville on October 15, 1903. The *Xenia Daily Gazette*, (Dr. Gee was originally from Xenia), described the event as "A Swell Wedding in Colored Society." As a wedding present, Nelson had a home built for the Gees on South Fifth St. in Zanesville. Dr. Gee practiced medicine from his office in that building.

Lulu died from what was described as tubercular meningitis at age twenty-four in 1905, just a few months after Nelson died. The Gees are buried at Gant Circle in Woodlawn Cemetery.

Lavinia died in 1912 and is buried in Gant Circle of Woodlawn Cemetery.

Gravestone of Lulu and Dr. Gee on Gant Circle of Woodlawn Cemetery

The Home

A search of Muskingum County records has failed to reveal when the house was built. There are conflicting accounts. The common assumption seems to have been that Nelson "built" the house in the 1850s. According to the Muskingum County Recorder's records, Nelson purchased the property on which the home stands from the widow of Charles Converse in August of 1865. An article by Norris Schneider indicates that "When Gant bought the farm, a brick house stood on it. He remodeled the house several times during his life." [26]

Other articles indicate that he built the house.

A Falls Township 1852 Tax Map showing Pataskala Place as the property of Charles Convers.

LIFE IN OHIO 57

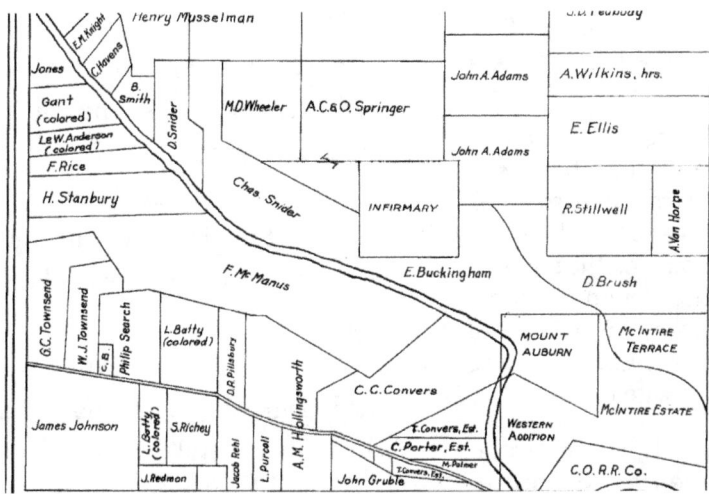

A Falls Township 1854 Tax Map showing Charles C. Convers as the owner of Pataskala Place and showing the land that Nelson purchased from John Dillon, up the river.

A March 1864 advertisement offering Pataskala for sale by Catherine Convers, widow of Charles C.

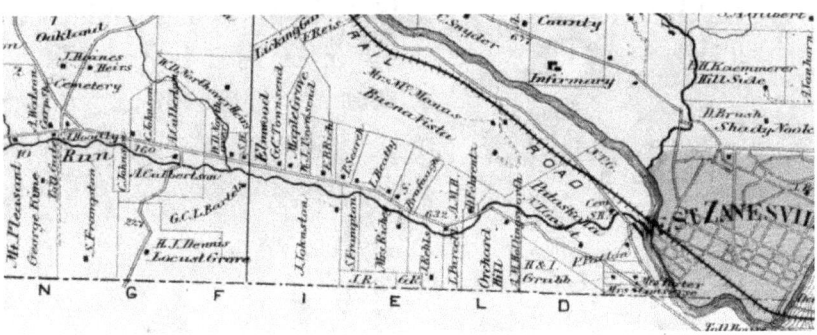

A map from the 1866 Muskingum County Atlas, showing N.T. Gant as the owner of Pataskala.

Whether Nelson built the home or purchased and remodeled it, he definitely put his stamp on it and made it Maria's and his.

One of the striking features of the home is the glass transom over the front door, engraved with the Gant name.

Over the years after Nelson died, ownership of the home passed through several hands. It was a restaurant and tavern in the 1930s. The Nelson T Gant Foundation purchased the home and began restoration in 2002.

The home is described in several articles as a "mansion." While it is well above average for its time, it would hardly be considered a mansion today.

When house numbers were assigned to residences on The National Road (West Main St), the Gant home was assigned the number 1845. Nelson may have influenced the number, as it is probably no coincidence that the house number matches the year, 1845, when he obtained his freedom.

History of the Home

My speculation, and it is just that, because I have found no solid evidence, is that there was a house on the property when Nelson purchased it from the widow of Charles Convers. I also speculate that:

1. Nelson and Maria rented a house from Charles (not Theodore), on the farm known as Pataskala Place, on the National Road. (a newspaper article about them selling strawberries and cream from a home on the National Rd, is dated 1854).
2. The rental home was on the first 35 acres that Nelson purchased from Catherine Convers in 1863. (The purchase price indicates that there may have been one or more structures on it).
3. The brick home on Pataskala Place became the Gant home after Nelson purchased it in 1865.

LIFE IN OHIO   59

Etched glass transom over the Gant Home front door.

Sketch of the Gant Home circa 1875.

Photo of the Gant Home 2023.

Land Transactions

Nelson, who as a slave was considered "property," became a property owner for the first time in March of 1853, two and a half years after arriving in the Zanesville area with 50 cents in his pocket. He purchased thirty-two acres in Falls Township, west of Zanesville. The property was purchased from John Dillon, for a total sum of $1,287, which amounts to $40.22 per acre. At the time, it was generally understood that a white man would not sell land to an African American, but Dillon was a Quaker and abolitionist and the land was of questionable value because it frequently flooded, so the transaction was frowned upon by some but not challenged. Dillon and Nelson became friends.

The next two transactions are probably connected, possibly involving a swap of land with a few dollars of "boot" (additional compensation). According to Muskingum County records, Gant purchased, from Howard Stanberry, 10 acres of land on September 16, 1853, for the sum of $1.00. Part of the description of this land indicated that it was adjacent to land owned by John Dillon and land owned by Theodore Convers. On December 27, 1853, Gant sold to Howard Stanberry a "tractor parcel" of land (no acreage specified), for the sum of $40.00.

It was a while before Nelson bought more land. In March of 1860, he purchased thirty two acres, adjoining his holdings, from Alvah Buckingham of Muskingum County and Solomon Sturgis of Cook County, Illinois. Buckingham was one of the abolitionists from Putnam. The purchase price was $1,500, $46.86 per acre.

In October of 1860, Nelson purchased another parcel from Stanberry. That transaction was for 30 acres, adjacent to the 10 acres he had purchased from Stanberry earlier. The purchase price was $500, $16.67 per acre.

Thus, by the end of 1860, after ten years in Ohio, Gant owned over 100 acres of land.

In October of 1863, Gant purchased thirty-five acres of land from Catherine Convers. Catherine was the widow of Charles, and thus a sister-in-law to Theodore, for whom Nelson had worked, and the sister of Alvah Buckingham, one of the prominent Putnam abolitionists. The purchase price was $3,580, $102.29 per acre, significantly higher than the $16.67 per acre he had paid Stanberry three years earlier. That may be because there was one or more structures on the land.

Nelson's first significant sale of land occurred in March of 1865. He sold eighty-three acres to John Talley for $3,911, $47.12 per acre. In the same month, he sold thirty-one acres to John Jordon for $2,490, $80.29 per acre. These sales were probably transacted in anticipation of his purchase of more of the Catherine Convers land. Nelson apparently leased out the land involved in these transactions, for in both deeds the wording stipulates that the current crops on the land did not convey, but were the property of a William Steed.

A purchase of seventy-four acres from Gilbert Parmer occurred in May of 1865. Nelson paid $3,000 for that land, which was $40.54 per acre.

An 1852 tax map shows Pataskala Place owned by Charles Cleveland Convers. Charles died in 1860. In March of 1864, Catherine ran an advertisement in the *Zanesville Daily Courier* indicating that she was offering for sale a Beautiful Farm known as Pataskala Place. No acreage is specified.

On August 26, 1865, Nelson purchased another one hundred seven acres from Catherine Convers, the widow of Charles. He paid $11,000 for that property, which was $103.77 per acre, if the transaction included only land. Deeds of the period did not specifically identify structures but referred to them as "appurtenances." This deed, (a copy of which is included as Appendix D) makes three references to "Appurtenances thereto," which may refer to one or more structures on the land.

Map of land Nelson purchased from Catherine Convers, widow of Charles.

In 1866, Nelson sold sixteen building lots to William Graham for the sum of $3,500.

Nelson was a shrewd businessman. In 1877, he apparently saw an opportunity to buy and "flip" a significant piece of property. On August 20 of that year, he purchased from Francis McManus, a citizen of Chihuahua, Mexico, two hundred fifty acres of Muskingum County land. He paid $10,500 for the parcel. According to Muskingum County records, Francis had purchased the land from his mother, Jane McManus, a resident of Muskingum County, for $10,000 in January of 1855. It is interesting to consider how difficult it must have been to close a transaction for Ohio land with someone in Mexico. The signatures of Francis McManus and his wife, Concepcion, were witnessed in Chihuahua, Mexico by John C. Huston, Vice Counsel of the United States and by Abraham Eriberto Perez, *Escribano Publico,* (Notary Public).

The interesting language in the description of the property, typical of the times. includes the following:

"... from which a Black Oak, eight inches in diameter, bears North 85 degrees, East 16 links distant, and a Dogwood, 4 inches in diameter bears North to East 15 links distant."

(It would appear that if someone needed firewood and removed one of the trees, the property line would have come into question.)

Less than two months after making the purchase, Gant sold those two hundred fifty acres, on September 13, 1877, to Nicolas Dantz for $15,000. The $4,500 profit was not a bad return on his investment.

On May 2, 1878, Nelson purchased three building lots in the "Riverside" section of Zanesville from Mary Porter for $800. Less than a month later, he sold one of the lots to Jesse Beatty for $275. In Oct of 1879, he sold the other two lots to Jackson Smith for $1,200. His net profit of $675 represented a nice return on his $800 investment. He seemed to know what he was doing.

Outside of the purchase of the Gant homestead, perhaps Nelson's most important acquisition occurred in April of 1881. He purchased 147 acres on Ridge Road in Springfield Township, southwest of Zanesville, from David and Marietta Bumgardner, for $8,200. This purchase proved fortuitous for it was on this land that Nelson developed the coal mine that added significantly to his subsequent wealth.

Part of the property in Falls Township, near the home, was a wooded section that became known as Gant's Grove. It evolved into a popular picnic spot and gathering area for local citizens.

Map of Springfield Township land Nelson purchased, on which his coal mine was located.

Francis Townsend, who owned the local mule drawn trolley company, saw an opportunity to increase the traffic on his streetcars. He leased the property from Nelson in 1888 and established an amusement park. The park included a pavilion, picnic grounds, a dance hall and a baseball field. It was one of the first integrated parks in the state of Ohio. The ball field was later developed into Municipal Stadium and has since been renamed as Gant Municipal Stadium. After the amusement park closed, the grounds hosted the Barnum and Baily Circus and Buffalo Bill's Wild West Show.

It was not uncommon for trolley companies of the period to build parks to stimulate traffic. The enterprise, named Gant Park in honor of Nelson and Anna Maria, opened in April of 1888. The Zanesville newspaper printed the following account:

> Gant Park is to be thrown open to the public today. Manager Townsend said yesterday that in order to provide for the comfort of patrons of the streetcar line, he would arrange for the sprinkling of the West Side Track, so as to lay the dust.

The newspaper account of the opening appeared the following day:

> In the afternoon, Bauer's band headed a procession of city and county officers in an excursion over the Street Railway to the park.
>
> After a charming musical program, spirited addresses were made by F. M. Townsend, president of the Street Railway, Captain B. F. Power, prosecuting attorney, W. S. Bell, president of city council, and R. H. McFarland, city solicitor. The speakers, on behalf of the city and county governments, endorsed the enterprise.
>
> Last evening, the park was thronged by a delightful crowd. Bauer's band furnished the music and the merry dancers indulged in callisthenic exercises until a late hour.
>
> The opening and dedication of the Main Street and West Side Railway and Gant Park was a brilliant success.

Photo of Mucci painting of the entrance to Gant Park, circa 1892.

A later article made the observation that the horse and mule cars immediately began hauling passengers to the new park. It was not a fast or comfortable means of transportation but was a little better than walking.

After leasing the land from the Gants for two years, Townsend purchased the twenty-two acres in June of 1890. The purchase price was $20,000, which was $909 per acre, for land for which Nelson had paid less than $105 per acre in 1863 and 1865.

The park was a popular place for community gatherings. *The Zanesville Times Recorder* printed an account of one such gathering on June 27, 1901:

> *The members of the Old Maids' club believe in reciprocation (even if they do not believe in marrying), as their entertainment of the Bachelor's club for supper last night is ample evidence. The members of both clubs went to Gant Park on the car and there the Old Maids, as hostesses, furnished an appetizing supper to their jolly bachelor friends.*
>
> *The Bachelors, after partaking of the delightful repast furnished them by the Old Maids, spoke seriously of repealing section 17 of their bylaws, which forbids marriage.*

Subsequently, Nelson bought and sold some building lots, but completed no other major land transactions.

(Accounts of Gant's real estate transactions are taken from copies of deeds in the Muskingum County Recorder's office).

Businesses

Nelson's primary business was growing and selling fruits and vegetables. He understood supply and demand and niche marketing. He was also an entrepreneur who developed additional businesses.

Nelson's first entrepreneurial efforts are referred to in an article printed in the *Zanesville Courier* in June of 1854. The reporter relates that one can enhance a pleasant walk or ride by stopping at the N.T. Gant residence on the National Road for strawberries and cream, which will be served in good style and at reasonable prices.

Accounts indicate that he specialized in early varieties from the farm, for which he could get premium prices. He was especially known for his strawberries, and is credited for developing a tasty variety of cantaloupe, called the Dresden Melon. He and Maria also sold milk and cream from their cows, and raised livestock on the land in Springfield Township.

The constitution of the State of Ohio prohibited slavery within the state's borders. However, it would be naïve to think that Nelson's experiences with prejudices ended with his move to a free state.

Zanesville had a market house or "farmers market" at which local producers sold their goods directly to consumers. When Nelson attempted to obtain a space in that marketplace to sell his produce, he ran into resistance from the white stall owners. In time, he won them over and purchased the stall.

An article in *The Freeman*, an Indianapolis publication that described itself as "An Illustrated Colored Newspaper," recounts this incident in his business life:

> *Everything was closed to Gant, on account of color. His indomitable will and persistence began to open the way. He purchased a small farm and began its work. Mob violence was threatened him if he attempted to purchase a stall at the market house. His determination soon quieted the mob and the stall was purchased.*[27]

Nelson built a frame "ice house" on Timber Run Creek, which flowed into the Licking River, and insulated it extensively with sawdust. He and his crew cut ice on the creek and on the Licking

River in the winter and sold it from the ice house in warmer months. The foundation for the ice house is all that remains.

Foundation of the Ice House on Timber Run, the only remains of the structure from which Nelson sold ice.

Probably the most profitable of Nelson's ventures was the coal mine on the land he purchased in Springfield Township. The document titled Biographical and Historical Memoirs of Muskingum County Ohio indicates that: "the land, located about two and a half miles from the city, was devoted to stock raising as well as coal mining, the yield being ample to help supply the citizens of Zanesville as well as the surrounding county with coal."[28]

Nelson also sold salt from a "salt lick," on his property, of which the exact location is uncertain. Some accounts place it near the ice house, others on the Springfield Township property near the coal mine.

Nelson did not work all the time, especially in his later years. An article in the *Zanesville Times Recorder* for January 25, 1900, was written to defend the sport of hunting, especially quail hunting.

Nelson's name was included with other prominent businessmen and politicians who enjoyed hunting. The Sale Bill for Nelson's goods and chattels, recorded on November 23, 1905, includes the sale of one shotgun to Robert Manley for the sum of $12.75.

At various times. Nelson managed from eight to ten employees in his four businesses—the farm, coal mine, salt lick and ice house.

Several newspaper articles refer to Gant as a "millionaire." The article announcing that Governor Bushnell had appointed Gant to represent Ohio at the Tennessee World Exposition, names: "Nelson T. Gant, the Zanesville millionaire."[29]

A summary of his will was published in the *Zanesville Times Recorder* on July 19, 1905. It indicated that the estate was conservatively estimated at $100,000. Of course, $100,000 was a lot of money in 1905, but somewhat short of a million. Nelson was a generous man. Accounts indicate that he purchased, or had built, homes for his five adult offspring. He gave generously to his church, including $5,000 for a building campaign. An estate of $100,000 is impressive, considering that he started with 50 cents at age twenty-nine.

Contributions to Church and Community

Nelson became a highly respected citizen of Muskingum County and his adopted state. He served his community well. He was one of the founders and a trustee of Zanesville's first community hospital, which later became known as Bethesda Hospital. The *History of Muskingum County*, identifies N. T. Gant as one of the incorporators of the Zanesville City Hospital Association, the purpose of which is:

"1st, to provide medical and surgical aid and nursing for sick and disabled persons, free of expense to those unable to pay, and at a cost to those who are able to pay... 2nd, to instruct and train suitable persons in the duties of nursing and attending upon the sick... This corporation is not created for profit, but will rely for its establishment and support, on the voluntary gifts of the charitable and humane."

Nelson was also a trustee of Woodlawn Cemetery in Putnam, at the behest of his friend A. A. Guthrie, who was the designer and director of that cemetery.

According to an article in the *Zanesville Times Recorder*, on May 3, 1895, Gant was selected to serve on a special Grand Jury, appointed by the Court.

The Gants generously shared their good fortune with citizens of the community. The wooded area dubbed Gant's Grove, before he sold it to Townsend, was frequently used by locals as a picnic area and the site of civic events. He and Maria also hosted strawberry socials at their home.

Nelson was a trustee and steward of the African Methodist Episcopal (A.M.E.) Church on South Street in Zanesville. When that church conducted a campaign to construct a new building, Gant contributed $5,000 of the $7,000 total cost. In the twentieth century the building became too expensive to maintain and the A.M.E. Church moved to a new location. The South Street site is now a city parking lot.

331 South Street

The African Methodist Episcopal church on South St. in Zanesville, of which Maria and Nelson were active members and for which they provided the bulk of the construction cost.

Gant served on the Board of Trustees of Wilberforce University in southwestern Ohio. His association with the A.M.E. Church put him in contact with Daniel Payne, who was the American Bishop of the denomination and a "major shaper" of that denomination for forty years. Payne was an ardent advocate of education. He started several schools and was one of the founders of Wilberforce University.

The web site of the University relates the following history:

> *Wilberforce University is the nation's oldest private, historically black university owned and operated by African Americans. Its roots trace back to its founding in 1856, a period of American history marred by the physical bondage of people of African descent. It was also a period when the education of African Americans was not only socially prohibited but was illegal. There was nothing about the prevailing social and cultural ethos of the era that suggested that African Americans might or should be taught or could learn. Yet a powerful idea assumed life and Wilberforce University was born. The founding of Wilberforce University represented a bold, audacious and visionary example of what could happen when men and women of goodwill transcended race and the prevailing social and cultural constructs and norms to pursue a noble purpose.*
>
> *Wilberforce University was named for the great eighteenth century abolitionist, William Wilberforce who said: 'we are too young to realize that certain things are impossible. . . so we will do them anyway.' It was this can-do spirit that infused Wilberforce University with strength to persevere, and the institution met with early success through 1862. The outbreak of the Civil War forced the school to temporarily close its doors. This short setback did not deter the institution for long. In March 1863, Daniel Payne, a Bishop of the African Methodist Episcopal Church, negotiated to purchase the land and buildings and the University was re-incorporated on July 10, 1863. Bishop Payne opened the doors of the University with six students and a debt of $10,000. He became the first person of African descent to be the president of an American institution of higher learning. Wilberforce University prospered as young African Americans sought to educate themselves as the ending of the Civil War promised a new social order.*

Payne convinced the A.M.E. church to buy the University in 1863, and Payne became president. He and Gant were friends, (Payne wrote a eulogy to Maria when she died), and Payne enlisted Gant to serve on the Board of Trustees at Wilberforce.

The African Methodist Episcopal church is a part of a worldwide Council of Methodist Churches. That organization held its first Council of the World Conference at Wesley Chapel in London, England in September of 1881. The stated purpose of the meeting was to review and refine the ideals and doctrines of the Methodist Church worldwide. Both Gant and Payne were selected as delegates from the United States. The *Indianapolis Leader* (newspaper) ran an article on September 17, 1881 as follows:

> *The following names comprise a full and complete list of the colored delegates from this country to the Methodist Council of the World, now in session at London, England.*

Rev Bishop Daniel Payne, DD Wilberforce, O
Bishop J. M. Brown, Washington, D. C.
Bishop James A Shorter, Wilberforce, O
Bishop Wm. F. Dickerson DD, Columbia, S.C.
Rev B. T. Lee DD, Wilberforce, O
Rev James M. Townsend, Richmond, Ind
Rev Augustus T. Carr
Rev James C. Embry, Leavenworth, Kan.
Mr. Alexander H. Clark, Iowa City
Prof. Joseph P. Shorter, Wilberforce, O.
Mr. Nelson T. Gant, Zanesville, O
Mr. Joseph W. Morris, Cokesbury, S. C.
Bishop J. W. Hood Fayetteville, N. C.
Bishop S. T. Jones DD, Washington, D. C.

This conference, which lasted for twelve days, was attended by some 400 delegates from around the world. During the conference, the delegates were hosted by the Lord Mayor of London at a reception in the Mansion House.

In *The Doctrines and Discipline of the AME Church*, the minutes of the meeting of the General Conference of the African Methodist Episcopal Church, held in Columbus Ohio on May 7, 1900, state that Nelson was elected to the Board of Trustees for the Denomination. That Board of Trustees consisted of four Bishops, four Ministers and four Laymen. The list of duties included "management of endowment and other funds and to take charge of, manage, rent, lease, improve, sell or otherwise dispose of, all real estate belonging to, or which might be acquired by, the denomination."

Nelson and Politics

Nelson was active in politics as a member of the Republican Party, the party of Lincoln, most abolitionists, and most African Americans of the period. *The Columbus Dispatch*, on January 16, 1890, printed an article that indicated that Governor Nash was considering the appointment of Nelson to the trusteeship of a state institution. The reporter opined that if that didn't happen, Nelson Jr. might receive an appointment to a state job, as reward for Nelson Sr.'s service to the Party. (Nelson Jr. was later appointed by the governor to a position in the State Department of Insurance.) The same article indicated that Congressman Van Voorhis, of the fifth district, depended on Nelson to reach all his people in Zanesville politics.

The Freeman, a colored newspaper published in Indianapolis, ran an article on September 25, 1897, reporting that "a Mr. McSimpson and Nelson T. Gant, one of the wealthy colored men of the state, were in Columbus in consultation with the Republican State Committee."

Nelson's political involvement apparently extended to a level beyond Muskingum County and Ohio. The *New York Age* was a weekly newspaper founded in 1887, by Timothy Thomas Fortune, a former slave. It is described as the most prominent African American newspaper of its time. While the name, *New York,* appeared in the paper's masthead, the publication regularly included articles from multiple states about issues considered of interest to the African American community. In a column labeled "National Capital Topics," an article about discussions on the floor of the House of Representatives, concerning race, appeared in the issue dated January 20, 1891. The correspondent for Washington DC noted in that article that Nelson Gant of Zanesville, Ohio was in town. The fact that Nelson is mentioned in the same article with the discussions in the House of Representatives may imply that Nelson was there to participate or observe. He doesn't explain who Nelson is or why he is in the nation's capital. That could be because of an oversight, lack of space, laziness or, perhaps, because he thought his readers would know who Nelson was. In any case, he thought it was newsworthy that Nelson was in Washington, DC.

Ohio Governor Bushnell appointed Nelson Gant as one of the delegates to represent Ohio at the Tennessee Centennial and International Exposition at Nashville in 1897, (a predecessor of subsequent "World Fairs"). President William McKinley officially opened the event and the featured speaker on "Emancipation Day" was Booker T. Washington, president of Tuskegee Institute. Attendance to the six-month-long exposition exceeded 1,786,000 persons.[30]

An Exchange of Letters

Nelson Gant's principles, values and character, including the attributes of gratitude and loyalty, are illustrated by an exchange of letters between Gant and an African American political group. These letters were reprinted in several newspapers around the state of Ohio, as well as one in Wheeling., West Virginia, including:

Marietta Daily Leader—Oct 19, 1897
Steubenville Daily Star—Oct 18, 1897
Hillsboro News Herald—Oct 18, 1897
Akron Beacon Journal—Oct 19, 1897
Wheeling Intelligencer—Oct 20, 1897

The letter sent to Gant:

Mr. Nelson Gant, Zanesville, O.

Hoping that you will not consider us inquisitive, we desire that you send us an answer to the following questions:

Do you hold that Governor Bushnell is to blame for the Urbana affair? If so, are you willing and ready to take an active part (quietly) in opposition to his ambition?

Don't you believe the wrong committed at Urbana should be rebuked by defeating those officials of the law who are candidates for re-election and are in any degree responsible for the violation of law and order at Urbana June 4, 1897?

We are not fighting the Republican Party, therefore we are not in favor of the Negro ticket. We are opposed, first, last and all the time to Bushnell being re-elected governor. The law-and-order element in the Afro-American League of Republican Clubs of Franklin County, Ohio are at the head of this movement.

Hoping that you will assist us and that we may receive an answer by return mail, we remain,

Yours for justice,

J. J. Lee, Chairman
W. T. Thomas, Secy.

Gant replied as follows:

Zanesville, O., Oct. 7, 1897

J. J. Lee, Chairman, etc.

SIR: I am in receipt of your circular letter of October 2, and in reply to your first question will answer: I do not hold that Governor Bushnell is to blame at all in the Urbana affair.

In reply to your second question will say: 'I will take no part whatever in any effort to defeat Governor Bushnell; on the other hand, I will do all in my power to elect him to the position for which my party has nominated him.

To your third question will say: I am not informed that the sheriff and city officials of the city of Urbana are candidates for re-election. If they are, I think they should be defeated.

I may state further that I possibly have given the whole Urbana matter more attention and investigation than many so-called Republicans who propose, by their actions, to defeat Governor Bushnell and thereby defeat the party that has been the only real political friend my race ever had in this country. Besides, I find by impartial investigation that Governor Bushnell has all his life been a real friend to my kind, from the time when the underground railroad, of which he was a part, was the only way we had to liberty; also that he has been one of the few white men in this great country that has stood by my kind, giving them equal chance with the whites to earn a livelihood by employing them in his workshops.

No, gentlemen, I would be ungrateful to the party that you say you are not fighting, ungrateful to my Creator, ungrateful to my race, and would deserve the severest condemnation that my kind could put upon me, God forbid that I should so much as turn my hand over to hurt our real friends.

May I say further that when you gentlemen play into the hands of our enemies, as I take it you are now doing, you are fighting me, you are inflicting injury upon yourselves and upon your race. Let me beg of you to cease your effort or you will see the day you will regret it.

Yours in justice,
N. T. Gant

(note the irony of using the similar closing phrase)

The "Urbana Affair," mentioned in both letters, refers to the lynching of an African American man, Charles "Chick" Mitchell, in Urbana, Ohio on June 4, 1897. Mitchell was accused, tried, and convicted, in an Urbana court of raping a white woman. He was sentenced to twenty years in the Ohio penitentiary and remanded to the local jail to await transport. Overnight, a mob broke into the jail, removed Mitchell, beat him severely and hanged him by the neck from a tree in the town square, until he was dead.

That this incident occurred in Ohio in 1897 is just one of a multitude of instances that illustrate that the plight of African Americans did not end with the Emancipation Proclamation in 1865. Research by the NAACP indicates that at least 3,446 African Americans were lynched in the United States between 1882 and 1968.

Respect

Through sterling character, hard work, and personal achievements, Nelson earned the respect of friends and associates, those who knew him and those who knew of him. He was selected by area citizens to serve on the Board of Trustees in the formative years of the local hospital and on the Board of Woodlawn Cemetery. The Governor of Ohio selected him to represent the state at the Tennessee World Exposition. His church chose him to lead as a member of the board and as a steward. His denomination chose him to represent all the churches in the denomination at a World Conference in London. A university selected him to contribute to the education of young people as a member of the board of trustees. His opinions and thoughts were sought and valued by many.

He earned a reputation not typical or likely for someone who spent his first twenty-three years as a slave.

The following are but *some* of the tributes to the character and contributions of this man among men who set standards to which we all might aspire:

TRIBUTES TO GANT'S ACHIEVEMENTS AND CHARACTER

Comment	Source/Occasion
"No man living is more devoted to his family and friends."	Biographical and Historical Memoirs of Muskingum County, Ohio. 1892
"He has always been deeply interested in the welfare of Zanesville and has done as much as any citizen in the county to further her interests. His career paints its own moral and has few parallels in the history of men of mark."	Biographical and Historical Memoirs of Muskingum County, Ohio. 1892
"By thrift and industry, the couple acquired a large farm and won the esteem of the Zanesville people"	*Zanesville Stories,* by Norris Schneider, 1965
"By industry and shrewd business ability, he became prosperous."	*Zanesville Stories,* by Norris Schneider, 1975
"Death has removed from this community one of the most remarkable men in our history. He stood and will stand in a class by himself. He never had a prototype here and there cannot be another like him."	The Zanesville Courier, July 1905
"What he was and did remains to teach and inspire. His life shows conclusively that poverty is no real barrier to success."	The Times Recorder. July 17, 1905
"Gant's friends and relatives will remember that by toil and thrift he rose from slavery and poverty to freedom, honor and wealth, by demonstrating unconquerable will, tireless industry, sound judgment, keen mentality and true, fine and solid character."	The Times Recorder, editorial July 1905.

LIFE IN OHIO   79

"His life was characterized by many sterling traits, prominent among which were unfaltering diligence, unquestioned integrity, and faithfulness to every trust reposed to him."

PAST AND PRESENT of the CITY OF ZANESVILLE and MUSKINGUM COUNTY By J. Hope Sutor. Chicago, 1905.

"Mr. Gant is a man of robust appearance, very sociable and a great lover of his race; an interesting conversationalist and a Christian gentleman. His life should be an inspiration to youth of both races."

The Freeman: An Illustrated Colored Newspaper. Feb 3, 1900

"They may recount with especial pleasure the obstacles which he overcame in that upward march; for everything that is recalled takes full measure of the unconquerable will, the tireless industry, the sound judgment, the keen mentality, the true, fine and solid character, which lay back of it all."

Lewis Lemaster. The Zanesville Times Recorder. June 3, 2017.

"His struggle from slavery to prominence is forever worthy of emulation."

Earnell Brown. The Zanesville Times Recorder. Oct. 20, 2000

N. T. Gant was perhaps the most remarkable colored citizen of Muskingum County. His labors won for him the success which his upright character so well deserved.

The Zanesville Signal. July 15, 1905

He had lived here for more than a half century and was a familiar figure to every citizen in the city. During his more than 55 years of residence in the city he was a gardener and for his products was known throughout the county.

The Zanesville Times Recorder. July 15, 1905.

The career of this colored man who escaped from slavery, is an object lesson that thousands of white men of the North might take to themselves greatly to their advantage.

The Sandusky Register, July 21, 1894.

Nelson earned the respect of the white community, (the comments above are all by white writers), and he was especially highly regarded in the African American community of the Zanesville area.

An event in 1866 illustrates the respect with which he was held. He was selected for the position of "President of the Day" for the community celebration of the anniversary of The Emancipation Proclamation. The following is a transcript of an article that appeared in the Zanesville newspaper:

> *Colored People's Celebration—The celebration by the colored people of this City and vicinity to-day, of the anniversary of President Lincoln's Emancipation Proclamation, passed off very nicely.*
>
> *The procession, as it passed down Main and Seventh streets, and after marching through a number of streets, headed to Gant's Grove, where the speaking took place this afternoon. The orator of the day was Frederick Douglas.*
>
> *The procession as it passed along down Main street was marshalled by Charles Adams, followed by Atwood's Band, then followed by the President of the Day, N.T. Gant, Vice President Charles M. Proctor, and Chaplain, Elder J A Warren, all in a carriage. Following was a carriage containing Frederick Douglas, the orator of the day, and J. McSimpson, Secretary.*
>
> *In front of each carriage was a copy of the proclamation, framed and neatly twined around with evergreen. Then came a wagon with all little girls dressed in white. Following this was a long procession of carriages and wagons.*
>
> *The whole affair was the finest display our colored people have ever made in this city. This evening, Frederick Douglas lectures at Nevitt's Hall.*[31]

It was during this visit to Zanesville that Douglass was a guest at the Gant home.

Putnam and Abolition

The Emancipation Society of Putnam was formed in 1831 and became the Emancipation Society of Muskingum County in 1833. The leaders of the Abolitionist movement included the Guthrie brothers, Albert Austin, George, and Stephen, as well as Horace Nye, Lucinda Belknap Nye, Goodsel Buckingham, Alvah Buckingham, Levi Whipple, Matthew Gillespie, Adam Francis, H. C. Howell, and William Harris. All were active participants in the Underground Railroad. The homes of several of these abolitionists, as well as the Stone Academy, were Underground Railroad "stations."

In 1833, monthly prayer meetings beseeching the end of slavery commenced, first at the Stone Academy and subsequently at the Putnam Presbyterian Church.

The Stone Academy in Putnam, built in 1809, was the site of the state convention for the Abolitionist Society of Ohio in 1835. The 1839 convention met at the nearby Putnam Presbyterian Church. On both occasions, pro-slavery mobs from Zanesville invaded Putnam and disrupted the meetings. In 1835, the mob burned two barns where the horses of out-of-town visitors were sheltered. Theodore Weld, a noted anti-slavery lecturer, was the featured speaker at the 1835 convention. Weld related that "A mob came, broke the windows and doors, tore off the gate and attacked me when I came out with clubs and stones. . . ."

When the meeting at the Stone Academy was interrupted by the mob, the group adjourned to A. A. Guthrie's home to continue. When members of the mob followed Guthrie home, he thanked them for the "escort."

During the 1839 meeting, a mob of over 200 from Zanesville and the surrounding area, disturbed by the convention, threatened to burn all of Putnam. One group had brought a bucket of tar and feathers intended for H.C. Howells, but he escaped and climbed a

The Stone Academy in Putnam, the site of 19th-century abolitionist activities and which now houses the Putnam Underground Railroad Interpretive Center.

Sign outside the Stone Academy.

The A. A. Guthrie home in Putnam.

tree from which he watched the mob searching for him. The intruders were met and repelled by a group of armed defenders labeled the "Putnam Grays." The leader of the Zanesville mob and several of the participants were arrested and jailed. Several of the mob, to avoid apprehension, swam back across the river.[32]

The Putnam Presbyterian Church was one of the centers of abolitionist activity in the area and a station on the Underground Railroad. A. A. Guthrie, whose home was just down the street, was one of the founders and a ruling elder of the church. The first pastor of the church, when it was built in 1835, was William Beecher. William was the brother of Harriet Beecher Stowe, the author of *Uncle Tom's Cabin*, the book some credit with causing the Civil War. That credit, according to American folklore, derives from Abraham Lincoln's comment when he received Stowe at the White House. He allegedly stated, as he shook her hand; "So this is the little woman who made this big war." Stowe visited her brother and the church on more than one occasion. She traveled nationally and internationally speaking about her book and the evils of slavery. She was one of the several abolitionist speakers at the Putnam church.

Putnam Presbyterian Church, site of 19th century abolitionist activities.

William was also the brother of Henry Ward Beecher, a famous abolitionist pastor of a large church in Brooklyn, New York. Prayer meetings addressing the abolition of slavery were held monthly in the church basement for several years, and the church hosted several meetings featuring abolitionist speakers, the most notable being Frederick Douglass, who addressed an audience there on two occasions. Nelson met Douglass at one of those meetings.

The town of Putnam was annexed into the city of Zanesville in 1872.

Nelson and the Underground Railroad.

Although Nelson didn't live in Putnam, he had friends in the village and was active in the abolitionist activities that were centered there. The current brochure for the Putnam Underground Railroad Interpretive Center states that: "UGRR operatives Nelson T. Gant and Joshua M. Simpson were leaders of an extremely active African American population."

The Underground Railroad wasn't a railroad, nor was it underground. It was a racially integrated civil rights movement that involved white people and Black people cooperating in an effort to provide justice to a group of humans who were being deprived of their basic human rights. The participants broke the law, risking their lives, fortunes, and freedom to save the lives of thousands and change the lives of tens of thousands. While doing so, the participants accomplished the greatest social/political feat in American history.

The objective of the movement was to provide aid to any freedom seeker who requested it. It was truly a grass roots effort. As one Ohio "station master" related, there was no regular organization, no constitution, no officers, no written laws or agreements, no rules, except the Golden Rule, and every man did what seemed right to him.

The "railroad" was a loosely organized local and regional system of "safe houses" where freedom seeking slaves could find food and shelter. Histories of the period provide multiple descriptions of secret rooms and false walls to facilitate the hiding of freedom seekers.

Trapdoor in a closet of the Stone Academy through which freedom seekers accessed the hiding space under the building.

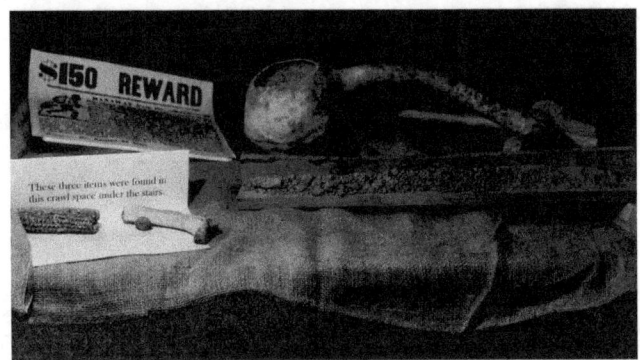

Items found in the hiding space under the Stone Academy.

Volunteers guided refugees, and often provided transportation, to the next "station." The railroad was "manned" by brave men and women –free blacks, slaves, and white abolitionists, allied in an effort to help freedom seekers find safe havens in Canada or the free states.

Historians, who have studied the UGRR, estimate that the system enabled between 100,000 and 150,000 slaves to find freedom between 1800 and 1865. Perhaps one-third ended up in Canada, which had abolished slavery in 1834. Because what they were doing was illegal and secretive, there are no accounts of the number of persons directly involved in the UGRR, but the number was surely in the thousands.

The abolitionist movement and the UGRR forced Americans to face a moral dilemma, and led them to expect those in government to consider the moral implications of their decisions. The efforts of those involved changed America dramatically. Whites and Blacks discovered that they could effectively collaborate if the cause was "right."

One of the most famous of the Underground Railroad stories is that of Elisa Harris, the subject of the poignant and most memorable episode in Harriet Beecher Stowe's novel *Uncle Tom's Cabin*. The episode is based upon actual events. Those events are described by Levi Coffin, a station master on the Railroad, who is often referred to as the "President of the Underground Railroad," because of his extensive involvement in, and commitment to, helping slaves reach freedom.

In his memoir, Coffin relates the events as described to him by Elisa:

> *I will give a short sketch of the fugitive's story as she related it.*
>
> *She said she was a slave from Kentucky, the property of a man who lived a few miles back from the Ohio River, below Ripley, Ohio. Her master and mistress were kind to her, and she had a comfortable home, but her master got into some pecuniary difficulty, and she learned that she and her only child were to be separated. She had buried two children, and was doubly attached to the one she had left, a bright, promising child, over two years old. When she found that it was to be taken from her, she was filled with grief and dismay, and resolved to make her escape that night if possible.*
>
> *She watched her opportunity, and when darkness had settled down and all the family had retired to sleep, she started with her child in her arms and walked straight toward the Ohio River. She knew it was frozen over at that season of the year, and hoped to cross without difficulty on the ice, but when she reached its banks at daylight, she found that the ice had broken up and was slowly*

drifting in large cakes. She ventured to go to a house nearby, where she was kindly received and permitted to remain through the day. She hoped to find some way to cross the river the next night, but there seemed little prospect of anyone being able to cross in safety, for during the day the ice became more broken and dangerous to cross.

In the evening she discovered pursuers nearing the house, and with desperate courage she determined to cross the river, or perish in the attempt. Clasping her child in her arms she darted out of the back door and ran toward the river, followed by her pursuers, who had just dismounted from their horses when they caught sight of her. No fear or thought of personal danger entered Eliza's mind, for she felt that she had rather be drowned than to be captured and separated from her child.

Clasping her babe to her bosom with her left arm, she sprang on to the first cake of ice, then from that to another and another. Sometimes the cake she was on would sink beneath her weight, then she would slide her child on to the next cake, pull herself on with her hands, and so continue her hazardous journey. She became wet to her waist with ice water and her hands were benumbed with cold, but as she made her way from one cake of ice to another, she felt that surely the Lord was preserving and upholding her, and that nothing could harm her.

When she reached the Ohio side, near Ripley, she was completely exhausted and almost breathless. A man, who had been standing on the bank watching her progress with amazement and expecting every moment to see her go down, assisted her up the bank. After she had recovered her strength a little, he directed her to a house on the hill, on the outskirts of town. She made her way to the place, and was kindly received and cared for.

It was not considered safe for her to remain there during the night, so, after resting a while and being provisioned with food and dry clothing, she was conducted to a station on the Underground

> *Railroad, a few miles farther from the river. The next night she was forwarded on from station to station to our house in Newport, where she arrived safely and remained several days.*
>
> *Other fugitives arrived, in the meantime, and Eliza and her child were sent with them, by the Greenville branch of the Underground Railroad, to Sandusky, Ohio. They reached that place in safety, and crossed the lake to Canada, locating finally at Chatham, Canada West.*[33]

Because of its proximity to Kentucky and Virginia, Ohio was a major conduit of the Underground Railroad. The Ohio River became symbolic of the gateway to freedom. A map of some of the most traveled routes is shown in Appendix E.

Albert Austin Guthrie, Nelson's benefactor and associate, was referred to by Wilbur Siebert, the noted Underground Railroad historian, as "the most fearless station agent and conductor."

Hudson Ward, a clerk in Guthrie's general store, recounted that:

> *fugitive slaves would come to the door of the store... Mr. Guthrie would supply them with shoes or clothing, whatever they needed, and then help them right on.*[34]

A, A.'s brother George and his wife were also active in the Railroad. In her unpublished autobiography, George's wife recalls that she remembers hiding three children in their attic while their owners were searching the streets for them.

Nelson had a reputation as one of the active "conductors" on the Railroad. He was reputed to feed and shelter slaves in the basement of his home and to transport them to other "safe houses," hidden in his produce wagons. Such activities were necessarily secretive and there is little, if any, specific documentation. These activities were in violation of the Fugitive Slave laws and were thus conducted at great risk. The risks came not only from government authorities, but from pro-slavery zealots. Because of their activities in assisting fugitive slaves, two African American brothers in Berlin Cross Roads, Ohio were killed by slavery supporters.

Nelson regularly violated federal law and accepted the associated risk; by doing what he thought was right and aiding runaways in their quest for freedom.

The article in *Ohio History Central* about Nelson begins with the statement:

> Nelson Gant was a former slave and a conductor on the Underground Railroad.

Tribute to Nelson T. Gant, displayed on the wall of the Putnam Underground Railroad Interpretive Center.

One of the stations to which Nelson likely transported freedom seeking slaves was the Prospect Place mansion of G. W. Adams in Trinway, Ohio, fourteen miles directly north of Nelson's home.

G. W's father had sold his plantation in Virginia, near where Nelson was born, and moved to Ohio, because he was opposed to slavery. G. W., like his father, was an ardent abolitionist and was well-known as an activist in the

A likeness of Nelson T. Gant displayed on the wall of the Putnam Underground Railroad Interpretive Center.

Underground Railroad. Abolitionist meetings were held at Prospect Place in the 1840's, 50's, and 60's. Like Nelson, G. W. was active in the Republican Party. A plaque in the Trinway home and the written history of Prospect Place, both mention that Nelson T Gant was a guest in the home.

Prospect Place, an Underground Railroad Station in Trinway, Ohio.

In her book titled *The Underground Railroad In Ohio*, Kathy Shultz refers to Gant as a successful hider of fugitive slaves.

The National Park Service's *National Underground Railroad Network to Freedom* recognized the Gant home as an Underground Railroad site in 2004 and placed a commemorative plaque in the front yard.

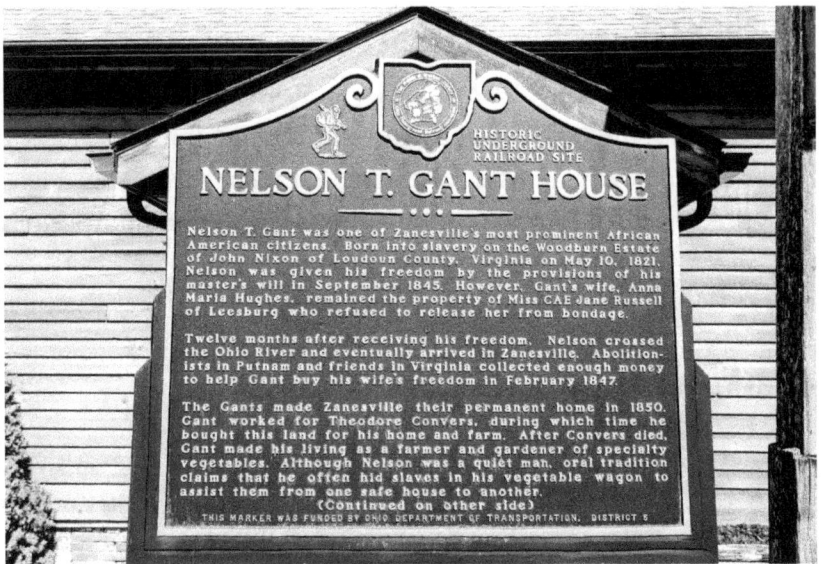

Plaque in front of the Gant Home, recognizing it as a National Park Service National Underground Railroad Network to Freedom site.

Civil Disobedience

Nelson was not a rebel and had great respect for just law and order. However, he was no stranger to civil disobedience. He, at times, felt an obligation to comply with a "higher law" and to do what was right rather than what was legal. He probably learned to read and write while a slave, which violated Virginia state law. When Maria's mistress refused his offers to purchase Maria's freedom, he conspired with Maria to run away. He stayed in Virginia longer than the allowed twelve months because he felt an obligation to work off his debts to people there. After moving to Ohio, he assisted the former enslaved in their search for freedom, in violation of the Federal Fugitive Slave Laws.

Timeline

Nelson died on July 14, 1905.

A list of some of Nelson's farm tools and equipment sold at a public auction on November 23 of that year is shown in Appendix F.

A timeline of the major events in Nelson's life is shown in Appendix G.

Gant Descendants

An interview with Victoria Robinson, Nelson and Maria's great-great-great granddaughter, which addresses what the Gants' legacy means to their descendants, is transcribed in Appendix H.

A family tree, developed by Ms. Robinson, is shown in Appendix I.

Life Lessons

VALUES, PRINCIPLES, and CHARACTER

There is much we can learn about how to live a meaningful life by reflecting on and applying the lessons revealed by the Gant story.

Nelson Gant overcame obstacles and recorded significant achievements because of the person he was, and because of his character. He consciously and rationally chose to live a life that was productive, meaningful, and satisfying, while modeling integrity, and concern for others. He lived that kind of life because he aligned his thinking and actions with the principles and values that represent the time and experience tested collective wisdom of humankind.

Values are those standards and qualities we deem to have inherent worth and which we consider deeply important. Values shape decisions and decisions shape lives. Decisions that are the easiest, the most convenient or the most personally beneficial are not always the "right" decisions. Choices, which are effective and with which we can live comfortably, must be consistent with our core values. If our behavior is not consistent with our values, we will feel dissatisfied with the results, uncomfortable, and out of sync with the world. When our actions are consistent with our values, we are much more likely to achieve positive outcomes and be more satisfied with our choices.

> *Carefully watch your thoughts, for they become your words. Manage and watch your words, for they become your actions. Consider and judge your actions, for they become your habits. Acknowledge and watch your habits, for they become your values. Understand and embrace your values, for they become your destiny.*
>
> *Mahatma Gandhi*

Decisions about personal values are some of the most important decisions we ever make. They determine the kind of person we become. Once established, they should serve as guides for making other important decisions. Our values should provide an internal compass that guides the roadmap of our life journey. To determine if a decision is "right," we should test possible choices against our values. To test a decision against our values, we must have previously considered and defined our ethical and moral standards and what core values are really important to us. That requires careful thought and is something that should be done with deliberation and great care before we are faced with the pressure of making an important decision. By deciding now what is important, we will be better prepared to align our actions with our values in times of crisis or change.

With every decision you make, you are writing the story of your life. Strive to make yours a story of which you can be proud and which has meaning.

In thinking about the values that are important, the following are some of the questions you should consider:

- How do I define right and wrong?
- What do I consider to be my moral absolutes?
- How do I define ethics in dealing with people?
- What do I consider to be my basic personal responsibilities?
- What are the qualities I admire about people I respect?
- What makes me feel fulfilled and proud?
- What values were involved in decisions I regret?

Values imbue our lives with meaning. Our values define who we are and who we want to be. They often involve making choices about what is right and wrong and what is the responsible thing to do under the circumstances.

Principles are concepts that govern human decency and effectiveness, natural laws in the human dimension that are just as real as natural laws in the physical dimension, (such as the law of gravity). Sound principles are based upon sound values, e.g. the principles; "I will not lie, cheat or steal" are based upon the value of integrity.

Character determines self-respect and the respect with which we are regarded by others. Character is determined by how we resolve the inner conflict between what is self-serving and what is right. Character is built by being dependable in times of testing, honest in times of temptation and compassionate in response to the needs of others. Personal values and principles are the foundations of character.

Nelson demonstrated these strong traits that we should attempt to incorporate into our personal characters:

Morality and Ethics

Morality is about how we treat people. Right decisions are those that resolve issues, while demonstrating respect for the rights of others and concern for their needs. There is much evidence and many testimonials that indicate Nelson was moral and ethical.

Honesty/Integrity

Being honest means not cheating, lying, or stealing. Nelson was very successful in his businesses. He sold fruits and vegetables, coal, salt, and ice. That he was successful means that customers came back, which indicates that he treated them fairly. He was repeatedly asked to accept positions of responsibility in organizations, which indicates that peers considered him an honest person.

Respect for Human Dignity

This concept holds that all people have intrinsic worth and certain "unalienable" rights. Nelson was denied those rights and that respect in many ways over many years, yet there is no evidence that he tried to "get even" or demonstrate malice towards those who denied him and others those rights and respect. He earned respect by conducting himself with integrity, compassion, and dignity.

Compassion

Nelson understood that people matter and that we should be ever aware of the impact of our actions, words, and decisions on others. At great personal risk, he demonstrated compassion for refugee slaves by helping them escape to freedom. In many ways, he exhibited a father's deep compassion for his offspring.

Kindness

The attribute of kindness encompasses being attentive, considerate, generous empathetic, and friendly. It involves listening to and helping others. It means showing care for others in a multitude of little ways. Nelson's strawberry socials for friends and his sharing of Gant Grove with the community were but two examples of his and Maria's kindness to others. Payne's eulogy of Maria emphasizes her kindness.

Responsibility

No matter how good or bad our decisions are, we are responsible for the consequences. We are responsible for our thoughts, beliefs, values, words, choices, and actions. We are responsible for how we treat other people, for keeping our promises, for our lives and personal well-being. Blaming others or finding excuses does not change that reality. We should not blame our circumstances on someone else's actions or on the "system." Accepting responsibility is the first step to finding solutions. Nelson took responsibility for his life, decided to change it, and made something special of it.

Conscientiousness

Literally, being conscientious means following one's conscience, doing what is right, developing a strong value system, and living by those values. Conscientiousness also means more. It means being dependable, doing what you say you will do, and being there for others, demonstrating that you are someone on which others can depend. It also means caring about the quality of the work one does. The myriad of responsibilities that Nelson was asked to take on in the community indicates that he was recognized as a conscientious person. That he worked hard to repay the money borrowed to free Maria and for his legal assistance demonstrated his conscientiousness.

Fairness/Justice

Fairness is the principle upon which our whole system of justice is based and on which the foundation of our understanding of what is "right" is grounded. Fairness is the principle upon which meaningful relationships are built. When injustice prevails, it is not because everyone approves, but because too few have the courage to openly disapprove. Nelson treated customers and others fairly and had the courage to oppose the injustice of slavery.

Tenacity

Being tenacious means having the mental and moral strength to endure adversity and pursue an objective in the face of opposition and hardship. It signifies persistent determination and an unwillingness to accept defeat. Nelson was tenacious in his attempts to free Maria and in his efforts to provide a secure and comfortable life for his family.

Quality/Excellence

Perfection is not possible, but striving for perfection improves results and makes a difference. Nelson did many things well and cared about the quality of what he did. Those who purchased from him were obviously satisfied that he provided a quality product, since they became repeat customers. He apparently provided value to the boards on which he served, since he continued as a member and was asked to take on additional responsibilities.

Meeting Commitments

Doing what we say we will do earns us the trust and respect of others, along with a clear conscience. Failing to meet commitments betrays others and ourselves. Nelson borrowed money to free Maria. By so doing, he made a commitment to repay. He stayed in Virginia, at great risk to his freedom, to pay off his debts there. When he got to Ohio, he paid off his debt to Guthrie.

Humility

Humility is the awareness that we are not the center of the universe; that we are here to serve a larger purpose and to serve others. It reminds us that we are not omnipotent, but interdependent, that we need others. Nelson recognized these realities. He relied on friends for help and spent a great deal of effort serving others.

Goodness

Goodness is not a word that gets used a lot. It's an encompassing word. When we say someone is a "good person," it is an indication of respect for who she/he is and how he/she lives. It refers to an inner orientation to do what is right, to serve others and to demonstrate integrity in every aspect of life. A truly good person is one who:

- Looks beyond personal interests
- Is not arrogant, brash or proud
- Focuses on what is important
- Seeks cooperation and unity rather than divisiveness
- Helps the vulnerable
- Includes the outsider
- Seeks healing rather than harm
- Seeks fairness and justice for all
- Seeks and speaks the truth
- Refuses to be controlled by anger and bitterness
- Recognizes the beauty and goodness that surrounds us

When adversaries attempted to deny Nelson a place in the farmer's market, he did not fight them. He won them over through his determination and persistence, but also because they realized that, despite the color of his skin, he was a good person.

Gratitude

One of the takeaways we should glean from the Gant story is that there is no such thing as a "self-made" man or woman. We are all influenced by the generosity and commitments of others, and thus owe a debt of gratitude. Gant demonstrated outstanding personal character, but his achievements were not entirely his own. He received a lot of help from others.

Eve Gant became a surrogate mother and helped instill into Nelson, life-affirming values and principles. Mothers shape lives. John Nixon, for whatever motives, exposed him to education and educated people and taught him business and management skills, which served Nelson well in his later endeavors. Nixon had a huge impact on Nelson's life by freeing him and the other Nixon slaves in his will.

Thomas Nichols loaned Nelson money and convinced John Janney to defend him in his trial for "stealing" Maria, and after the trial provided housing and employment. John Janney was instrumental in getting Nelson acquitted. Samuel Janney provided personal support, housing, and employment during the Gant's post-trial stay in Virginia.

Friends loaned Nelson the money to purchase Maria's freedom. A. A. Guthrie and other Putnam abolitionists, Nichols and Samuel Janney in Virginia, and perhaps others, contributed.

Guthrie, his brother, and other abolitionists in Putnam helped the Gants get settled and started in Ohio. Theodore Convers provided employment and taught Nelson the farm produce, growing and marketing business.

Gant demonstrated his gratitude in the most effective way, by thanking his benefactors, to be sure, and more importantly, by passing on compassion and generosity to others. He helped run-away slaves reach freedom, and helped others by supporting and serving a hospital, a cemetery, his church, and educational institutions. He provided employment through his businesses and modeled good citizenship.

> *If you concentrate on finding whatever is good in every situation, you will discover that your life will suddenly be filled with gratitude, a feeling that nurtures the soul.*
>
> Rabbi Harold Kushner

Courage

Courage is not the absence of fear. It means acting in spite of fear. Demonstrating courage means doing what is right regardless of personal danger, criticism, personal hardship, or popular opinion. Demonstrating courage includes confronting and attempting to correct injustice and unfairness.

It took courage for Nelson to return to Virginia to attempt to free Maria. It took courage for him to stay in Virginia to pay off his debts after Maria was freed. It took courage for him to risk what he had achieved by helping run-away slaves seek freedom. It took courage for him to succeed and build an exemplary reputation in a community where he was not a slave but regarded by many as a second class citizen because of the color of his skin.

Mold Your Character

Nelson demonstrated all of these worthy attributes of character. You would do well to emulate them. You cannot always control circumstances, but you can mold your character to deal with them more effectively.

Chose to Make Your Life Meaningful

In spite of a difficult beginning, Nelson lived a very responsible and meaningful life. You, too, can make your life meaningful. Seek wisdom and do the right thing. Wisdom is about more than thinking. It is choosing to live wisely, aligning actions with valid principles.

Life is an endless quest, a search for wisdom and for experiences that enlighten. Finding meaning and purpose takes effort, introspection and wise choices about principles and values. It means being open to direction from a Higher Intelligence, searching inside for the real you. It involves deciding what kind of person you choose to be and what kind of life you choose to live.

> *The value of life lies not in the length of days, but in the use we make of them; a man may live long yet live very little.*
>
> Michel Eyquem de Montaigne

In the end, meaning is very personal. We each have a responsibility to determine a purpose for our lives that has significance for us. At least a part of that task is to develop ourselves into the most wise, moral, strong and loving persons we can be, and to live in peace with a clear conscience. At the same time, we must understand that a "good" life is a process, not a state of being. We cannot be perfect.

> *We are visitors on this planet. We are here for ninety, a hundred years at the very most. During that time we must try to do something good, something useful with our lives. Try to be at peace with yourself and help others share that peace. If you contribute to other people's happiness, you will find the true goal, the meaning of life.*
>
> *The Dalai Lama*

Let Your Life Speak

The way Nelson lived his life demonstrated what kind of person he was. Make your life an accurate picture of who you are.

The real you is not revealed by what you believe or what you profess, but by what you do. Let the way you live your life demonstrate who you are. Doing good enables you to be good and to feel good.

Commit to truth.
Practice Integrity.
Live ethically and morally.
Serve others.
Search for understanding and wisdom.
Treat the really important as priorities.
Treat people with kindness and compassion.
Support justice and fairness for all.

Choose to Live

Henry David Thoreau wrote that he wanted: "to front only the essential facts of life, and see if I could learn what it had to teach, and not, when I came to die, to discover that I had not lived."

He chose to live. So should you. The world is a wonderful and mysterious place. It offers more possibilities than we can ever conceive. Try some of them.

Make a decision to make better decisions. Making better decisions will improve the quality of your life. One of the most important, fundamental decisions that we can make is to decide to live our lives, not just take up time and space, but really live.

Imagine you only have ten hours to live. What would you do?
Imagine you only have ten days to live. What would you do?
Imagine you only have ten months to live. What would you do?

Contemplate your answers to these questions. What would you do differently if you knew the exact amount of life you had left? How would you redesign/refocus your life? Assuming that you would do something differently, why should not knowing the duration of your life keep you from starting that redesign now, from changing your focus now?

As Elizabeth Kubler Ross attempted to teach us, we do not know how much longer we will live, but we know our lives are finite. No matter the duration, we should live to maximize our relationship with family and friends, provide service and solace to others, and strive to live up to our potential. We should face the fact that we have but a limited time, and thus cherish it by living every day to its fullest

Develop a bias for action. Live life, don't just let it happen. DO SOMETHING to:

- Ease the burdens of others.
- Help others grow and realize their potential.
- Demonstrate kindness.
- Mold your character to align with valid principles.
- Learn, grow and realize your personal potential.
- Make something beautiful.
- Teach someone something useful.
- Promote social fairness and justice.
- Improve relationships between people.
- Preserve the wonder and beauty of nature.

It is in doing these things that we find meaning.

One of my favorite observations about life was written by George Bernard Shaw:

> *Life is no brief candle to me. It is a sort of splendid torch which I have got a hold of for the moment, and I want to make it burn as brightly as possible before handing it on to future generations. I want to be thoroughly used up when I die, for the harder I work, the more I live. I rejoice in life for its own sake. This is the true joy of life: being used for a purpose recognized by yourself as a worthy one, being thoroughly worn out before being thrown on the scrap heap, being a force of nature instead of a selfish little clod of ailments and grievances complaining that the world will not devote itself to making you happy.*

Every day do something to make you a better you. Every day, learn something new. Every day, demonstrate compassion for someone. Regularly ask yourself, am I becoming the person I want to be?

Life is precious! CHOOSE TO LIVE IT. This is not a rehearsal.

THE MEASURE OF A MAN

Humankind's greatest weaknesses are selfishness, greed, envy, fear, and hate. These weaknesses inhibit our ability to cooperate for individual and common good and to recognize and realize the potential of our interdependence. In his book, *The Measure of a Man*, Martin Luther King Jr. states that the real measure of a life is determined by the extent to which one is concerned about others, that one does not start living until one can rise above personal concerns to concerns for others.

Nelson Gant was very human. He had weaknesses common to us all, but he was able, on the whole, to overcome and rise above them. He overcame major obstacles and later devoted his life to the concerns and well-being of others.

King relates that there are three dimensions of life, and without the three being correlated, working harmoniously together, life is incomplete and falls short of its potential.

The first dimension is concerned with developing inner power (character). The second dimension is the extent to which we are concerned about and attempt to help others. The third involves seeking and discovering God, without whom, life is meaningless, but with whom we are able to rise above the depths of despair to heights of hope.

I think that King would say that Nelson "*Measured Up.*"

Nelson T. Gant died of a heart attack in July of 1905, at age eighty-four. He was a hero to only a few. He never won a World Series with a home run or hit a three-pointer to win an NBA title. He never became an astronaut or the president of a nation. But, by strength of character, rational decisions, prodigious effort and dogged persistence, he achieved many small triumphs over the adversities inherent in being born Black in America, and modeled a life well lived.

NOTES

1. *Registered In The Chancery of Heaven.* Blog by Victoria Robinson. November 27, 2009.

2. Interview with Victoria Robinson, January 14, 2023.

3. Jones, Thomas H., *The Experience of Thomas H. Jones, Who Was a Slave for Forty-three Years.* Boston. Bazin & Chandler. 1862.

4. Grandy, Moses, *Narrative of the Life of Moses Grandy: Late a Slave in the United States of America.* London. Gilpin. 1843.

5. Northup, Solomon, *Twelve Years A Slave.* Auburn, NY. Derby and Miller. 1853.

6. Douglass, Frederick, *Narrative of the Life Of Frederick Douglass, An American Slave.* Boston, MA. The Anti-Slavery Office. 1845.

7. Ibid.

8. Henson, Josiah, *The Life of Josiah Henson, Formally a Slave, Now an Inhabitant of Canada, as Narrated by Himself.* 1849.

9. Blassingame, John W., *Voices From the Past.* Work Projects Administration. Ed 2017.

10. Northup, Solomon, *Twelve Years A Slave.*

11. Douglass, Frederick, *Narrative of the Life of Frederick Douglass, An American Slave.*

12. *Registered In The Chancery of Heaven.* Blog by Victoria Robinson. November 27, 2009.

13. The *Cincinnati Enquirer*, Tuesday, January 21, 1879.

14. Ibid.

15. The *National Era*, January 7, 1847.

16. Ibid.

17. Ibid.

18. Ibid.

19. Ibid.

20. Letters of Francis J. LeMoyne, Washington County Historical Society. 1847.

21. Recorded last Will of Theodore Convers.

22. *Registered In The Chancery of Heaven.* Blog by Victoria Robinson. November 27, 2009.

23. Tribute to Maria by Bishop Payne, printed in *The Christian Recorder*, April 11, 1878.

24. Letter to Nelson from Daniel W. Atwood, printed in *The

Christian Recorder, April 11, 1878.

25. *The Zanesville Daily Courier,* October 13, 1877.

26. Schneider, Norris F., *The Zanesville Signal,* April 14, 1946.

27. *The Freeman,* Indianapolis, February 3, 1900.

28. *Biographical and Historical Memoirs of Muskingum County, Ohio.* Chicago. The Goodspeed Publishing Co. 1892.

29. *The Cleveland Plain Dealer.* March 12, 1897.

30. Tennessee State Library and Archives.

31. *The Zanesville Daily Courier,* September 21, 1866.

32. Suter, Hope, *Past and Present of the City of Zanesville and Muskingum County, Ohio.* Chicago, 1905.

33. Coffin, Levi. *Reminiscences of Levi Coffin, the Reputed President of the Underground Railroad; Being a Brief History of the Labors of a Lifetime in Behalf of the Slave, with the Stories of Numerous Fugitives, Who Gained Their Freedom Through His Instrumentality, and Many Other Incidents.* Second Edition. Cincinnati, OH. Robert Clark and Company. 1880.

34. Ward, Hudson Champlin, Letter to Wilbur Siebert, 10 September, 1895.

APPENDIX A
Nelson T. Gant's Freedom Papers

PARTIAL TRANSCRIPTION OF THE ABOVE

Virginia To Wit

    I Charles G. Eskridge, Clerk of this County Court of Loudoun, and state aforesaid, do hereby certify that Nelson Talbut Gant is a free person of colour, emancipated by the last will and testament of John Nixon, dec. ... by the direction of Ely Janney & Thomas Nichols two ... of said Nixon dec. The said Nelson T Gant is about twenty three years of age, five feet 9 ¾ inches high. He is a bright Mulatto with no particular scars or marks was this day registered in my office according to law. 9th Sept, 1845.

APPENDIX B
Slaves Manumitted by Nixon Will—Recorded in Loudon County Court, Sept. 9, 1845

Cert #	Name	Age
1333	**Gant, Nelson Talbert**	**aged 23**
1347	Gant, Eve	aged 53
1335	Gant, George	aged 20
1338	Gant, Fenton	aged 22
1339	Gant, Daniel	aged 18
1352	Gant, Winefred Jane	aged 17
1353	Gant, Susan Ann	aged 14
1341	Gant, John William	aged 15
1342	Gant, Isaac	aged 9
1343	Gant, Lloyd	aged 8
1354	Gant, Mary Frances	aged 2
1334	Talbert, Ely	aged 28
1344	Anderson, Sarah	aged 70
1345	Anderson, Eliza Ann	aged 30
1340	Anderson, Wilson	aged 29
1336	Anderson, Abraham	aged 26
1346	Anderson, Mary Ann	aged 11
1337	Jackson, Lewis	aged 25
1348	Adams, Harriet Ann	aged 27
1349	Adams, Virginia	aged 4
1350	Adams, Sally Ann	aged 2
1351	Adams, Amanda	aged 5 mo

APPENDIX C
Nelson T. Gant Jr.'S Letter to His Classmates in 1931

The O. C. '89 Class Letter
May 1931

Nelson T. Gant

Columbus, Ohio
February 19, 1931.

Dear Classmates:

I can hardly realize the many years that have elapsed sinces I left Oberlin. When I look back over the pleasant days spent there in preparation for a life of usefulness it seems but yesterday, so vividly do they appear.

I remember with pleasure having met several members of the class of '89 in Zanesville not so many years ago.

After leaving Oberlin I engaged in the business of gardening and farming with my father until my marriage when I assumed full control and continued in that line of endeavor until I left Zanesville to accept a clerical position in Columbus, under the administration of Governor "Geo." K. Nash, in 1900.

Was actively engaged in politics for many years. I remained as clerk in the State Department in Columbus until 1911. Since then I have been engaged in Real Estate and Farming.

> Remembrance is the sweetest flower
>   Of all this world's perfuming,
> Memory guards it, sun or shower,
>   Friendship keeps it blooming.

NELSON T. GANT.

APPENDIX D
Deed, Land—Convers to Gant 1865

APPENDIX E
Map of Underground Railroad Routes in Ohio

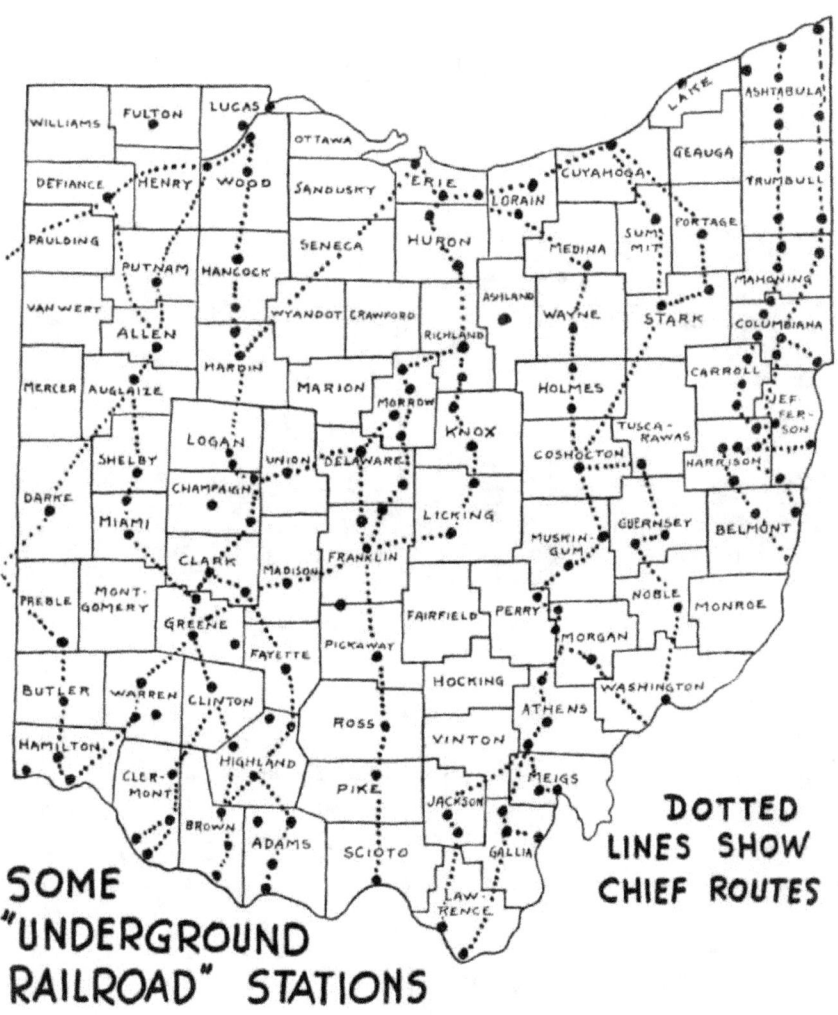

APPENDIX F
Sale Bill—Gant's Farm Tools and Equipment

SALE BILL.

Estate of _____ Nelson T. Gant _____ Deceased.

A Bill of the property sold by C. T. Marshall and N. T. Gant, Executors _____ the estate of _____ Nelson T. Gant _____ late ...uskingum County, deceased, at Public Vendue.

_____ November 23rd _____ A. D., 1905.

No. of Items	DESCRIPTION AS INVENTORIED.	Value as Inventoried.	TO WHOM SOLD.	PRICE.
1	Potato digger		R. F. Johnson	1.50
2	" "		Joe Dalton	1.75
3	Harrow		George Orr	1.00
4	Hay rake		C. L. Amspoker	.50
5	Old mower		J. M. Everett	.65
6	McCormick Mower		Geo. F. Brenner	10.00
7	Cultivator		" " "	.50
8	Harrow		" " "	2.00
9	Plow		" " "	.50
10	Cultivator		" " "	.70
11	Sleigh		" " "	1.00
12	Cultivator		J. M. Everett	1.50
13	Cultivator		Joe Dalton	2.50
14	Cultivator		George F. Brenner	.10
15	Plow		" " " "	4.00
16	Phaeton		Joe Dalton	3.50
17	Sulky plow		Geo. F. Brenner	1.50
18	Riding plow		" " "	2.25
19	Shovel and plow		R. F. Johnson	1.05
20	Wind mill		G. F. Brenner	.25
21	Set double harness		" " "	3.30

	Mattock	H. P. Miller	.15
24	Hoe	C. L. Amspoker	.10
25	Log chain	G. F. Brenner	.25
26	" "	J. M. Everett	.45
27	Old mower	G. F. Brenner	.70
28	Shot gun	Robert Manley	12.75
29	Disc Harrow	J. M. Everett	11.25
30	Drill	" " "	16.00
31	Wagon	Joe Dalton	22.00
32	Harness	G. F. Brenner	3.00
33	Cradle	" " "	.25
34	Grindstone	" " "	1.05
35	Brown mare	R. F. Johnson	39.00
36	Gray horse	J. M. Everett	19.25
37	Gray mare	Robert Manley	6.50

APPENDIX G
Nelson T. Gant Timeline—Summary

YEAR	Day/ Mon	Event	Notes
1821 or 1822	10-May	Nelson's Birth	1821 is the year most often recorded for Nelson's birth. His manumission papers, recorded in 1845, indicate an age of 23 yrs, indicating a birth year of 1822. Articles written at the time of his death in 1905, list his age as 84 years, indicating an 1821 birth year.
1826		Anna Maria's Birth	Date approximate - No record
1843	11-May	Anna Maria & Nelson Married	There is no official record. This is the date on which the couple celebrated their anniversery.
1845	Sept	Nelson freed by Nixon's will	
1846	12-Dec	Nelson tried for stealing his wife.	
1847	8-Feb	Anna Maria received her Freedom Papers.	Nelson purchased her freedom.
1847		Nelson & Maria worked for Nichols	To repay money Nichols loaned to Nelson
1848 - 50		Nelson & Maria worked for S Janney	
		First child, Mary Elizabeth born	

1850	Fall		Anna Maria, Nelson & Mary Arrived in Muskingum County
1853	12-Mar		Nelson purchased his first parcel of land.	32 acres from John Dillon.
1863 & 65			Nelson purchased land from Catherine Convers.	Land on which the Gant home resides.
1877			Maria died.	While visiting her daughter in Virginia
1879	Jan		Nelson married Lavinia Neal	In Wheeling.
1881	Apr		Nelson purchased 147 acres in Springfield Twp with a coal mine	From Bumgardner.
1881	Sept		Nelson selected to represent his denomination at the World Council of Methodist Churches in London, England.
1890	Jun		Nelson sold 22 acres to Townsend for Gant Park.
1897			Nelson selected to represent the State of Ohio at the Tennessee Centennial and International Exposition in Nashville.
1905	14-Jul		Nelson died.	At his home.

APPENDIX H

Transcript of Interview with Victoria Robinson, Maria And Nelson's Great, Great, Great Granddaughter

L: You've indicated that you have been researching the life of your great-great-great grandfather for many years. For how many years have you been doing that?

V: I think the very beginning was in 1982. I had rented a car because my sister was graduating from the coastguard and I was taking her to BWI airport. I decided that while I had the car I would drive out to Leesburg to look for the manumission records for Nelson and Maria. I found them in like five minutes, and then spent the rest of the day looking for stuff which I didn't find. So that's when I first started researching, like going and doing records researching. '82 would be forty one... oh my gosh... forty one years ago.

L: You are a descendant of which of Maria and Nelson's children?

V: Yes, I am a descendant of their daughter Margaret.

L: Now, I understand you are a genealogist by profession. Did you get interested in genealogy because of your interest in learning about Nelson Gant, or did you get interested in learning about your ancestor because of your interest in genealogy? Which came first?

V: Well, first of all, I am not a genealogist by profession. In a way I am, but my official work is with the Federal Government. I do volunteer, and teach people how to do genealogy and I give presentations at national, regional, and local genealogy conferences. I think I'm a genealogist because I am always interested in the stories. The stories I knew first were the ones involving the families of my parents. I remembered stories I heard when I was young. As a result of hearing family stories, learning about my ancestors, meeting real genealogists, and learning how to do genealogy stuff, I developed an appreciation for genealogy and the desire and passion to become a genealogist. So I guess it's because of my interest in my father's family, and later in Nelson and Anna Maria that my passion grew.

L: And what has the Gant legacy meant to your family over the generations?

V: Kids are not usually aware of that kind of thing, at least we weren't. I just took a lot of stuff for granted. College was taken for granted, things like that. The Gant family is a very small family of descendants. Over seven generations there might be a hundred of us living. As I was doing the research and learned more about his descendants, not only my line, but the sisters and brothers of my direct ancestors, I learned how they felt about education, about being proud of who had come before us and how they stood up to racism and oppression, no matter their complexion. Through DNA, I found the descendants of one of Nelson's great-granddaughters who we didn't know existed—basically we had lost track of her. Genealogy connected me to her great-grandson. And when I told him about the family history and that kind of stuff, he started crying, because he said 'I knew we were better than what we are.' His immediate family had issues in Chicago, but he'd always strived for more and now he recognized that it wasn't just him, that he had a family legacy. To me, that has been the most important thing that has come out of this. As I see it, helping the cousins who were unaware of that legacy find out about it, enabling them to explain and express what they felt internally, is the real value of the effort.

L: Wow, that's fascinating. And what do you hope that the Gant legacy will mean for your descendants? What would you like them to learn from that legacy?

V: That their future is up to them. That they have a voice—a strong voice—in deciding their own paths, defining those paths and taking them. I have two nieces, who I raised as my own. They're my sister's kids and I've had since they were three and five. They understand that—'You gotta go to college'. When the oldest one was writing her essay to go to college, she called the essay, 'The Seventh Generation'. She talked about being the seventh generation of continuous college graduates. At that point, I realized that she had been listening, and hearing those stories. I want them both to know that they can choose their paths much in the same way that Nelson and Anna Maria did. They forged their own path, against all odds they made decisions that were of benefit to them.

L: You mentioned that your mother is the oldest living Gant descendant. Are there stories about Nelson that have been passed down through the family?

V: Not necessarily from my mother, but from HER mother—my grandmother. My grandmother died in 2006. I used to go visit her every year. She lived in Minnesota. I'd go there, and she is the one who told me the stories when I was twelve or thirteen. I was told the story of Nelson Gant—that his mother died in childbirth... giving birth to him on the way up to the big house. That's how she phrased it—"on the way up to the big house."

She told me he was raised by another woman and that he stole his wife and then went to Zanesville and became very, very prosperous. Those were the basics of the stories that I heard. You know one of the things they always teach you when you're first learning genealogy is that not every story is true. I teach it a different way. I tell people not every element of the story may be true but there could be a basis for it, so don't ignore the family story. And so I use the stories I heard about him, primarily the trials and the tribulations that they had undergone, and how their kids had gone off to college and that kind of stuff—they went to Oberlin. That was how I learned what I did about Nelson and the descendants, by trying to prove or disprove the stories that I had been told. I found that every single story she told me turned out to be true. Knowing about what school they went to and about the money and the land and the like-led me to other stories—like him supposedly going to London as part of the Methodist Episcopal Conference. So those are the kinds of stories, for the most part, that I heard about Nelson and the family.

L: What would you consider to be the highlights of your search? Have there been any "Aha!" moments when you found something really striking?

V: Uh... "Aha!" moments... I guess the surprising thing for me about the Nelson and Anna Maria story, and getting to Zanesville, is the sheer amount of information available. I feel so blessed to have found so many records—state and local records, as well as newspaper records—that talked about them, you know, telling their story. People are like, "You found that?" Like the Virginia Governor's Extradition Order. In 1846 he extradited Nelson back to Loudon County for trial. Who would have thought that Nelson would be involved with the governor? So that was like a "Wow!" It did not give me an "Aha!," that I learned something new, it just strengthened the story I had been told. I guess the biggest "Aha!" would have been the people who defended him, who knew and helped him, like John Janney, who later on presided over the Virginia Secession Convention. He was a lawyer for Nelson in Nelson's trial in 1846. So, things like that I think were the biggest "Aha moments."

L: Have there been any real surprises in your search?

V: Not any surprises with Nelson. There might have been surprises with his grandsons. I learned of one's role in World War II and in the Korean War with the Merchant Marines. I think those were some of the biggest surprises I found. I also learned that a great-grandson filed one of the very first equal employment complaints under FDR's new Equal Employment Commission. The EEC was created to deal with the wartime industry. I literally stumbled upon that by doing just a blind search on newly digitized national archives records. He happened to be involved in one of the very first cases. That was a complete surprise to me, and I learned so much about him, and that time period, and what Kansas City was like in 1944-1945. So that was, I think, the biggest "Aha!" moment, like WOW! He died young, but worked in the war industry with Pratt & Whitney. I was just like, "wow, I never knew this about him." It was fascinating.

L: Is there anything you have looked for in particular that you've not been able to find yet?

V: What have I not been able to find? The confirmation of the number of children that Anna Maria had given birth to. Because this was before the formal civil registration of births and deaths in Ohio, information is scarce. I think that is one of the things I want to find out for sure, all the names of all the children that they had. Right now, I think I'm at about nine or ten, but I thought there were more. That's what I'm trying to get a sense of. I always wanted to find out more about Sarah Speed, who came from Lincolnshire as a thirteen-year-old white girl with her brother and the family, and became a servant to them as a teenager. She then stayed on as a member of the family. I want to know more about the story behind Sarah Speed and the Gants. I haven't found anything that talks about Sarah. She didn't have any kids, she never got married. She lived with the family for over forty years, and I don't know much about why, other than I think her parents sent the kids out to work on farms. That's all I know, but I always wanted to know more, because she was always called Aunt Sarah and she's buried in the Gant cemetery plot. I actually have a picture of her with Margaret, Nelson's daughter. I think Sarah was probably maybe at most ten years older than Margaret.

L: You have written and published several blogs about Gant. What motivated you to write those blogs?

V: I wanted to tell the story and I didn't want to lose it. I wrote it so I could send the link to my family to read. I wanted to learn more about the family in general and this was around the time that people were starting to do blogs about family history and stuff like that. So I saw it as a great and convenient way to have the story out there where it wouldn't get lost and the family could then point to it. When I found my cousin—the one from Chicago, I pointed to the blog so he could learn more. He thought he was the first one in his family to go to college. When he saw all that, he was like, "Wow." He hasn't graduated yet, but he has hopes and dreams and now he feels that he can do more because he knows about his legacy. That's what the blog thing was about—so people could read the story. That's why I wrote them and I wanted them to be real.

L: What kinds of reactions have you had from the family about the blogs?

V: They want to learn more. They want to hear more. They don't want to do the work, or course, but they want to learn more, so that in their minds, they know how people are in this family, how they're connected and stuff like that. Whenever I introduce them to family members, they're like, "Wow, Okay, great." So there's been, particularly with some of the younger generation, family connections made. My oldest is a fourth cousin to the young man in Chicago. and they're best buds now. They've never met, but they've been friends on the internet for ten years. They have a great relationship and discuss with each other what is going on in their lives. They're both parents of young children and they share their experiences. I also have never met him in person, and we've been friends for over ten years. So that, to me, has been a good benefit, to watch the next generation learning about each other. There aren't many of us, but we're all over the place.

L: You had mentioned that you had some personal DNA testing done to attempt to determine the identity of Gant's father. What did you learn from that?

V: I had always made the presumption that Nelson was the son, the biological son, of his enslaver John Nixon. Nelson was the first one listed in the manumission records. They usually do family groupings with the parents first, then the kids, and in that order. But, in this case, the very first one out of twenty one was Nelson Gant. He was not the oldest man. So I assumed that he was listed first because he was John Nixon's descendant. So the DNA has . . . I would say, almost verified the identity of Nelson's father. I'm still doing more research, but it's pretty much verified that I am a DNA match to a prominent white preacher from Leesburg. That ties into an article written in 1894 in which Nelson identifies his real father and indicates that he did not want to use his name because he was pro-slavery. I was expecting the article to say Nixon but it named this Methodist Minister as the father. Then when the DNA stuff started coming in it was like WOW, it actually did confirm this. So that's what the DNA did for me, and actually, the cousin in Chicago—he's also a DNA match to those same people. That showed me that, yep—we're on the right path. But

I have not reached out to that man's family at all. I haven't really felt the need to connect with them that way. But maybe one day I will.

L: There are lots of oral history stories about Nelson's activities in the Underground Railroad. Are there any particular family stories about that activity?

V: No. The only story that I heard about is that Nelson was a farmer/gardener, whatever, and that he drove a wagon and hid escaped slaves in his wagon. That was all I heard. Oh, Grandmother did tell a story about Nelson's house, which was near the Licking River, and that there was a tunnel from the basement of Nelson's house to the river, and they used that tunnel to hide the runaways and to give them a place to rest. I have heard about . . . I haven't verified that there was actually a tunnel, but . . . I was there . . . this would have been twenty six years ago. We went down to the basement and they opened up a section and we saw parts of a tunnel. It had been closed off or caved in, or whatever, so there's no way to tell if it is indeed true. So that was the only story that I heard about an Underground Railroad But you know he was there, and he was friends with the folks at Putnam . . . but people kept it quiet if they were involved in the Underground Railroad.

L: And how has the family reacted to his involvement in the Underground Railroad?

V: Oh, they smile . . . you know, they're like, "OH, Wow . . . Cool." They know that he wasn't just a jaded soul who was only after the money or that kind of stuff. When they learned about his role in the church, as a trustee, and how he started. . . he was on the Board of Trustees that created the cemetery that he's buried in, and how he interacted with people, they're proud of it. They're proud of it because, you know, sometimes you find out you have a very rich ancestor and you find out that... they might not have been such a good person. But they see from the stories that he was a decent person. But, what I think people don't realize, and one of the things I want to work on, is more about telling Anna Maria's story. She was his rock and he relied on her and her faith to keep him grounded. I think that's a story that needs to be told more—within our family—about her role and how she guided him and the kind of person she was. That was reflected in the obituary that Bishop Reverend Daniel Paine wrote in *The Christian Recorder* in 1877, about her passing. It tells her story and how Nelson got into the church because of Anna Maria. So the family's proud of it, you know, but it's like, okay there's an ancestor, but they're not going hog wild over it. They're proud of it, and they're glad they haven't heard anything negative about him.

L: What would you like people to understand about Nelson T. Gant?

V: Nelson was a man who, I think, grew into his prominence. He was a man who knew what he wanted. His biggest focus was that he wanted to get his wife—he was determined, and that he accomplished. Then he continued to set goals for himself that he would accomplish. But, he also recognized that he couldn't do it alone. He had friends and worked with them. He also made sure his children had the best. And so I think the most important thing is that he was a man, he was a human being, but he did a lot through his determination and the goals he set for himself and for his children. I think that's what made him a happy man in the end.

APPENDIX I
Gant Family Tree

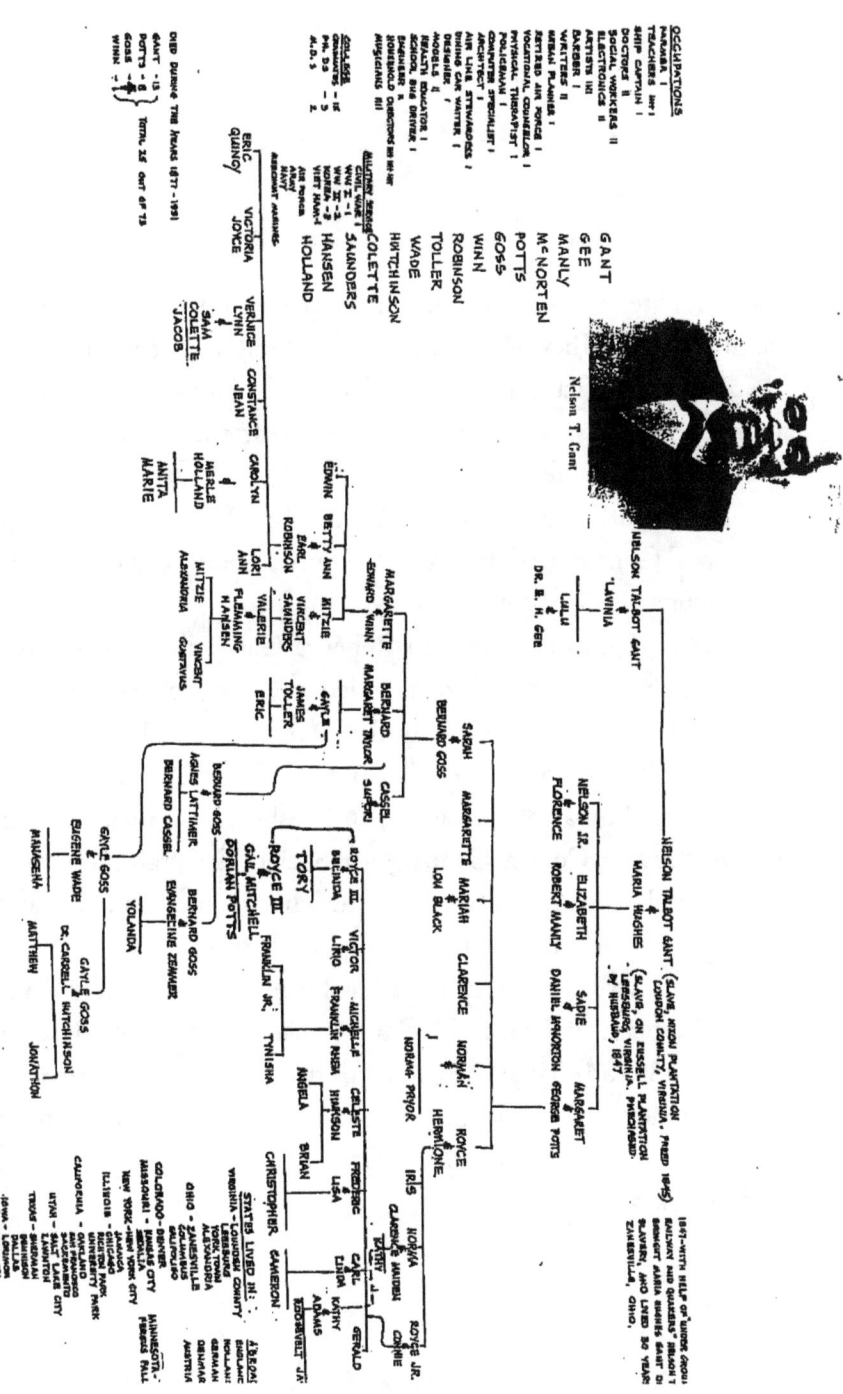

Acknowledgments

I am indebted to many people who contributed to this book in ways large and small. They made it better than it might have been. A special thanks goes to Victoria Robinson, Nelson T Gant's great-great-great granddaughter, who shared research and written blogs about aspects of her ancestor's life.

Steve Smith, President and Todd Ware, Vice President of the Nelson T Gant Foundation and the entire board of the foundation were supporters and contributors.

Special thanks also goes to Rebecca Carr who found valuable pieces of the puzzle which had eluded me. Research assistance. was also generously provided by Amy Goffee of the John McIntire Library in Zanesville, Marcie at the Muskingum County Recorder's Office, Sara at the Thomas Balch Library in Leesburg, Virginia, the staff at the Muskingum County Genealogical Society, Deborah at the Wayne County Public Library, Lucretia at the Muskingum County Records Center and Pete Cultice of Muskingum History.

As I am writing this story, it has been over two hundred years since the birth of Nelson T. Gant. Most of the events described occurred 130 to 180 years ago. Records from the period have gaps and inconsistencies and are sometimes sketchy. I have attempted to find the truth but cannot guarantee that I was always successful. Errors and mistakes are my own.

WILL YOU HELP?

This book was developed in conjunction with the Board of Trustees of the Nelson T Gant Foundation, which is a 501c3 non-profit organization. The Foundation is dedicated to building character, community and cultural pride, through educational and involvement programs and events modeled after the legacy of Nelson T. Gant.

If you can help with preserving the Gant legacy and helping young people learn the importance of developing appropriate values and principles, please send a tax-deductible contribution to:

Nelson T Gant Foundation
1845 West Main Street
P O box 3183
Zanesville, Ohio 43701

Bibliography

Biographical and Historical Memoirs of Muskingum County, Ohio. Chicago: The Goodspeed Publishing Co, 1892.

Bordewich, Fergus M. *Bound for Canaan, The Underground Railroad and the War for the Soul of America.* New York: Harper Collins, 2005.

Brooks, David. *The Road to Character.* New York: Random House, 2015.

Coffin, Levi. *Reminiscences of Levi Coffin, the Reputed President of the Underground Railroad; Being a Brief History of the Labors of a Lifetime in Behalf of the Slave, with the Stories of Numerous Fugitives, Who Gained Their Freedom Through His Instrumentality, and Many Other Incidents.* Second Edition. Cincinnati, OH: Robert Clark & Co., 1880.

Diouf, Sylviane. *Growing Up In Slavery.* Brookfield, CT: The Millbrook Press, 2001.

Douglass, Frederick. *Narrative of the Life Of Frederick Douglass, An American Slave.* Boston: The Anti-Slavery Office, 1845.

King, Martin Luther, Jr. *The Measure of a Man.* Philadephia: Fortress Press, 1988.

Kline, Stephanie & Wanda Bailey. *The Life and Times of Nelson T. Gant.* Zanesville, OH, 2003.

Lewis, Thomas William. *Zanesville and Muskingum County.* Chicago: S J Clarke Publishing, 1927.

Masur, Jenny. *Heroes of the Underground Railroad Around Washington, D.C.* Charleston, SC. The History Press, 2019.

Northup, Solomon. *Twelve Years A Slave.* Auburn, NY: Derby & Miller, 1853.

Pollard, Robert A. (ed.). *The History of the Loudoun County Courthouse and Its Role in the Path to Freedom, Justice, and Racial Equality in Loudoun County*. Leesburg, VA: Report of the Loudon County Heritage Commission, 2019.

Rudisel, Christine & Bob Blaisdell. Eds. *Slave Narratives of the Underground Railroad*. Garden City, NY. Dover Publications. 2014.

Schneider, Norris F. *Y Bridge City: The Story of Zanesville and Muskingum County*. Cleveland: The World Publishing Co., 1951.

Schneider, Norris F. *The Story of Nelson T. Gant*. Reprinted from the *Zanesville Sunday Times Signal*, April 4, 1946.

Schneider, Norris F. *Zanesville Stories*. "Zanesville Stories." *The Zanesville Times Recorder*, August 1965.

Siebert, Wilber H. *The Underground Railroad, From Slavery to Freedom, A Comprehensive History*. New York: MacMillan Co., 1898.

Schulz, Kathy. *The Underground Railroad In Ohio*. Charleston, SC: The History Press, 2023.

Sutor, J. Hope. *Past and Present of the City of Zanesville and Muskingum County*. Chicago: Clarke Co., 1905.

About the Author

LARRY SHIRER is a history buff, an author and a photographer.

He earned an MBA degree in Finance and Marketing from the Harvard Business School and a BBA from Ohio University. His 50+ year business career included serving as the Vice president and General Manager for a division of a New York Stock Exchange listed company and Vice President of Administration and Planning for a division of another NYSE listed company. During two stints as a management consultant, he helped owners and managers of many businesses improve the performance of their organizations. As a commercial real estate broker, he helped buyers and sellers, landlords and tenants negotiate sales and leases. He also owned, operated and sold two small businesses.

Serving as: Chairman of the Board of the United Way in one community, Chairman of the Allocations Committee of the United way in another community, Chairman of the Board of a soup kitchen, Chairman of a church's Strategic Planning committee, a member of a Homelessness Task Force and as a Mentor to junior high and high school youth, all contributed to his education, as did helping his wife rear five offspring and joyfully observing the rearing of nine grandchildren.

Larry has written and self-published seven previous books. The observations and life lessons advice in this book are based on the author's extensive experience and research in helping people get things done.

www.ingramcontent.com/pod-product-compliance
Lightning Source LLC
Chambersburg PA
CBHW050334010526
44119CB00004B/147